Organized to Last

PORTER BALL KNIGHT

DISCOVER
WRITING
PRESS

For information call Discover Writing Company 1-800-613-8055

or visit our website: www.discoverwriting.com

Cover and text by Bookwright Designs

Discover Writing Press

PO Box 264

Shoreham, VT 05770

1-800-613-8055

fax # 802-897-8024

www.discoverwriting.com

ISBN # 1-931492-07-7

Library of Congress Control Number: 2004112501

To my clients:
You honor me with your trust,
You amaze me with your creativity, and
You motivate me with your determination.
Thank you for encouraging me to write this book.

Contents

Organized by Knight's Just-for-Fun Stress Test

For each item, circle the symbol in the column that comes closest to categorizing your situation.

💣 **Always**   ☺ **Sometimes**   ☺ **Never**

1. I frequently lose track of things such as keys, wallet, and eyeglasses. 💣 ☺ ☺

2. There are items in my "To Read" pile that have been there longer than one month. 💣 ☺ ☺

3. Most of the time I seem to be rushing. 💣 ☺ ☺

4. Flat surfaces at home or at work (desk, shelves, credenza, filing cabinet) are covered in piles. 💣 ☺ ☺

5. There is more than one "junk drawer" in my house.

   💣 ☺ ☺

6. It has been over a year since I purged my files at home or at work. 💣 ☺ ☺

7. There are boxes in my home or office that have not been opened since I last moved. 💣 ☺ ☺

8. I have several broken items at home waiting to be repaired. 💣 ☺ ☺

9. My house is stuffed full of saved margarine containers, old envelopes, plastic bags, boxes, and the like. 💣 ☺ ☺

10. I have lots of unfinished "To Do" lists. 💣 ☺ ☺

11. I'm sure I have an extension cord (or several), but I don't know where. 💣 ☺ ☺

12. It's been years since I looked in my storage areas.

    💣 ☺ ☺

13. I lose phone messages so I miss vital calls. 💣 ☺ ☺

14. I make copies of things to file in several places to be sure I can find them again. 💣 ☺ ☺

15.   There's never enough time to do what I really want to do!

💣   😐   ☺

Scoring:

Mostly 💣: Time to get organized! Don't be discouraged—it's a skill you can learn!

Mixed 💣😐☺ or mostly 😐: It can get easier than this!

Mostly ☺: Enjoy your freedom!

1

What Does It Mean to Be Organized?

Betty contacted me about preparing for a move after attending one of my workshops. At 72, she was experiencing diminished mobility and was planning to transition to a retirement community. A former editor, she remained active in several local and national organizations, but the paperwork associated with them was weighing her down. When we began, the piles were stacked so thickly on the floor that there was just a narrow passageway from the door to the desk. After reclaiming the space, a remarkable thing happened. Betty, who had never married, received a call from her very first boyfriend, whom she hadn't spoken to since before World War II. Though they had corresponded during the war, she was away at college when he returned, and they lost touch. More than fifty years later, following the death of his wife, he began to look for her. They rekindled their romance and married. "All I wanted was to get rid of some of the clutter so I could prepare to move," said Betty. "But when I created all that openness, what came to fill it was totally unexpected. I think this relationship was made possible in part because I chose to let go of things that were holding me back."

There are as many reasons to get organized as there are people. Why do you want to get organized?

Here are some common reasons people cite for needing to get organized:

✓ I want my life to be balanced.

✓ I wish my spaces were clutter-free.

✓ I want to feel in control.

✓ I want to work more efficiently.

✓ I need to be able to find things easily (or quickly).

✓ I'm looking for a way to focus better.

✓ I want to have a home for everything.

✓ I want to have a plan for my day.

✓ I need to be able to meet deadlines.

✓ I like knowing where things are.

✓ I wish I were more frequently on time.

✓ I feel a need to create order in my life.

✓ I want to get more work done.

✓ I want to have more time for my loved ones.

✓ I want to be at peace with my surroundings.

✓ I want to feel energized, not drained.

✓ I want to be able to prioritize—reliably.

✓ I want to separate work space from living space.

✓ I'd like to have things shipshape.

✓ I'm trying to simplify.

✓ I want to have more time.

✓ I'm hoping to find time to do things I really want to do.

✓ I need to know what I can toss.

✓ I want to feel at all times that I'm on track.

✓ I want to use time effectively.

What is interesting is that people commonly define organizing by the results the organizing effort will produce. And the results each of us seeks are unique. Though we understand what others mean when they describe being "organized," we all have our own assumptions and expectations associated with the concept. Organizing is *personal*, and its definition is not the same for everyone. Though the dictionary defines *organize* as "to arrange into an orderly and functional structure or whole," trying to define *organization* in the real world is more complex.

You can't simply "become" organized by buying a fancy desk tray, reading a book, or hiring a professional organizer. Organizing is a *process*, not a one-shot deal. You must organize every day to build and maintain strong systems. Though you may sigh with resignation on hearing this, take heart—the fact that organizing is a process means that you have a new opportunity every day to work toward greater organization. Life is fluid, so organizing must also flow.

Finally, the purpose of organizing is a *specific result or set of outcomes*. Too often, organizing is confused with style or neatness. Organizing is not an end but a means to an end. Decide what you want to accomplish, and then organize your surroundings, possessions, and time to support your pursuit of those goals. How things look is not as important as how things work.

A holistic definition of organizing incorporates each of these three concepts: *organizing is a personal process that helps you achieve results.*

Melissa, a self-employed bookkeeper, decided it was time to organize when the spare room she used as a home office became overwhelmed with non-work-related junk. A bed, art and office supplies, memorabilia, wrapping paper, exercise equipment, books, electronics, and musical instruments were crowding out her small desk and table. As a result, she not only felt uncomfortable and unproductive in the room but avoided it altogether. Her goal was to create a functioning work environment and a quiet space to meditate. Together, we relocated the home office to an alcove off the front foyer and transformed the spare room into a yoga and meditation retreat. By eliminating unneeded items and sorting and storing the others, she was able to achieve her goal.

Richard manages a team of sales representatives for a software company. His responsibilities include supervising a staff of thirty-five as well as creating the department's budget and acting as a liaison between the marketing and research-and-development teams. Because he wanted to maintain an "open door" policy, he was constantly interrupted, frequently failed to meet deadlines on his projects, and had papers overflowing onto the floor from the pair of desks and the meeting table in his office. He had several organizing goals: (1) to improve the appearance of the office so that he could more easily find things and to present a more professional image,

(2) to manage his projects better so that they would be completed by their deadlines, and (3) to carve out blocks of time to focus on his work without sacrificing availability to his staff. By redesigning his filing system and office layout, improving his use of electronic and paper planning tools, and alternating open door time with quiet project time, he was able to meet all of his goals and set an example for his staff to follow.

Both Melissa and Richard continue to refine their systems to keep pace with incoming information and changes in roles and responsibilities. They know now that organizing is a personal process that helps them achieve their goals. They have to define their goals, set aside the time to develop a system, and maintain the system over time to ensure that it continues to meet their evolving needs.

What Organizing Is Not?

Organizing is not judgmental. You can organize yourself, but you should not try to organize other people, nor should anyone else tell you to "Get organized!" Because a sense of organization is subjective, you decide whether or not you are as organized as you need to be.

Organizing is not about appearances. As a professional organizer, I would never walk into a client's space and say, "Oh, boy, these people should have called me ages ago!" Nor would I walk into a client's space and say, "Well, this space looks OK—you don't need me." What other people see isn't necessarily related to whether or not you are organized.

Organizing cannot be equated with being uptight or compulsive. Organizing doesn't mean you are perfect either. Perfectionism and compulsive behavior diminish your ability to be productive. Once you are organized, you may still make mistakes. But you will take the time to prevent making the same mistake repeatedly.

2

Space, Stuff, Time:

The Three Gears of Organizing

The process of organizing involves the arrangement of space (rooms, desks and other flat surfaces, storage areas), the placement of stuff (information, paper, tools, and supplies), and the allocation of time (using lists and a calendar).

Space, stuff, time. These words are familiar but rarely considered and often confused. For instance, have you ever said to yourself, "This task is important. I have to do it. I'm going to leave the material out where I can see it"? If so, you probably found that you ended up with lots of stuff out, cluttering up your space. With nowhere to put the paper, tools, or supplies you need, you have to shuffle and stack other stuff to make room for the work at hand. All this creates tension and is not conducive to focused work. As a result, things pile up. They pile up on your desk, your counter, your shelves, the extra table or desk you brought in because your original desk was full, and so on.

Karrie is an educational consultant. She works out of her home, but her work has nearly displaced her from her home. The office at the far end of the house is bursting with paper, educational supplies, books and games, office supplies, office equipment, and student records. Every surface is piled high, including the three tables, small desk, dresser, bookcases, chairs, and floor. The chaos spills out from the office and includes the coffee table and end table in the living room, the entire dining room table, the large kitchen table, and a bookcase in the kitchen. Even Karrie's bedside table is heaped with reading material, and in the bedroom closet are baskets of reading material removed from the bedside table in months past when company was expected. Karrie knew she needed to get organized but wasn't sure where to start. "I have so much to do!" she lamented. "And I rely on all this information and these resources to provide service to my clients and schools. I don't have enough storage, and anyway, I'm afraid that if I put it all away, I won't remember to do it or won't be able to find it when I need it." Karrie is a good example of how people confuse the gears of organizing.

Here's what you (and Karrie) need to know about space, stuff, and time: they differ. They are not interchangeable. Using stuff as a time management tool—leaving it out, cluttering up your space—does not lead to organization. If you have a report to read, a tool to fix, or data to enter on the computer, leaving them all out on your desktop will not lead to their being read, fixed, or entered.

Instead, envision *open space,* stuff in a *safe home,* and a link to your *time system* for all the actions you intend to pursue. Your work space must be open, clear of clutter, so that you can focus on one task at a time in front of you without being distracted by all the other tasks you have yet to do. Your information, paper, tools, and supplies must be stored in safe homes where you can reliably find them when needed. And all of your actions must be recorded in a time system—some combination of lists and a calendar, to which you refer when deciding what actions to take at any given time.

Once she understood the gears of organizing, Karrie realized that she had covered her entire house with "things to do," making it hard to find a place to work and hard to concentrate when working. We started by defining a work area (a "hub") and creating open space in that work area. As we cleared the space, we created safe homes for the stuff, developed lists of all the things she has to do (including create more open spaces and other work hubs throughout the house), and scheduled time in her calendar to do them.

Space, stuff, time; the gears of organizing. If you remember to keep stuff, space, and time separate, they can work together. And when gears mesh neatly, they give you power, strength, and momentum to move forward and accomplish what you seek to accomplish. But if you confuse the gears, leaving stuff out to remind you to act, the gears jam and things pile up.

Keep these concepts distinct in your mind: Create open space. Put your stuff in safe homes. And create a link to your time system for all the things you have to do. Once you've got your gears engaged, it is time to FOCUS.

3

FOCUS on Getting Organized

The FOCUS principles lay the foundation for all organizing work. Depending on personal style and work flow, different individuals use different techniques and tools to organize their space, stuff, and time. But the FOCUS principles support the organizing effort of everyone in any situation. The FOCUS principles are as follows:

Forward thinking

Open space

Concentric circles

Upright storage

Simple systems

Forward Thinking

Forward thinking is a principle of organizing for two reasons. First, it feels good to move forward, to look toward the future. This principle can help you start the organizing process because keeping your eyes on the outcome of the organizing effort is a motivator that can help you overcome the fear of starting. Once you're in the midst of the organizing process, your positive progress is energizing and can help you stay motivated until you reach your organizing goal.

Seth hates filing. He is an energetic and ambitious lawyer for an advocacy group, and he is constantly in motion. Filing bores him. But he has discovered that he's much more effective when he can find the papers he needs in a snap. When he remembers to FOCUS on his goals, he can be motivated to put a paper away in the appropriate file before rushing to the next project. He thinks forward—past the boring task of filing—and anticipates the thrill of easily grabbing a complete file (without frantically digging through piles on his desk) when it is time to head out the door to trial.

The forward thinking principle also informs the placement of information and paper, tools, and supplies. People commonly put things away to make them go away. But that isn't really why we put things away. We put things away so we can find them again when we need them. So always think about the future when putting things away. Anticipate the next use of that object. Envision how, when, and where you will next need it. Put it away based on that future use—then you'll find it easily when the time comes.

Elijah had multiple sets of car keys because he frequently lost them. When his teenage sons started driving, all three of them chronically misplaced keys, resulting in several mornings of frenzied searches and late arrivals at school and work. They need the keys on the way out the door. So they put three hooks by the back door: one for each of them. And when they come in the door, they hang up their keys in tandem. They have developed a routine based on when and where they need the keys. Their FOCUS on getting out the door on time (with keys) helped them visualize where the keys should be placed and helps them maintain the discipline to place them there.

Open Space

Laura called one evening. "My in-laws are coming this weekend, but we can barely get in the guest room door because the room is so cluttered. Can you help?" For her family, the guest room had become the place to throw things they felt too busy to handle. But with guests on the way, it was time to organize. Once we cleared the floor so that the in-laws could actually walk from the door to the bed without climbing over anything, Laura was relieved.

It is easy to visualize the need for open space to allow physical movement in your guest room, office, kitchen, or garage. But it is just as critical to have open space on your desktop. If you have a project you need to develop, a letter you want to compose, or a report to write, you need to see the desktop—not stacks and stacks of other unfinished projects and miscellaneous paperwork hemming you in, distracting you. You'll be able to FOCUS on the task at hand with open space in front of you.

For that reason, do away with your blotter. Blotters were designed to protect the desk surface and to provide a place to "blot" ink from a pen. Unfortunately, blotters clutter the work surface and create a distraction. Thus they violate the FOCUS principles. Jotting something on a blotter doesn't move it forward, it embeds it on a flat surface. The blotter visually clutters the open work space of the desk, and it becomes a magnet for information and memorabilia. It becomes a scribbling board covered with all sorts of unrelated information.

Instead of writing on a blotter, store information in a file, Rolodex, or calendar. Move memorabilia to a visible vertical position or an archive box. If you like to make notes while you talk, keep a pad handy and scribble on it. But when you hang up the phone or finish the meeting, record actions in your time system and file necessary paperwork in a safe home. Then throw out your scribbles. The exercise of doodling is helpful as a way to engage your body and brain while listening, but don't keep those notes unless they propel you forward, in which case they should be filed appropriately, not left as clutter on your desk.

If you have a valuable wooden desk and you need to protect the desk surface, have a piece of glass cut to cover the entire desktop. If you need to blot your pen, keep a small piece of scrap paper near the inkwell or penholder. Either way, do away with the blotter.

Concentric Circles

I could see Jeremy's eyes light up when I explained the importance of open space and the energizing effect it would have on his work. His face fell, though, when he turned to his office and saw the mounds of drawings, awards, invoices, tools, notes, and magazines piled on the floor, desks, windowsill, and shelves. "I'd love open space!" he declared. "The question is, where does all that stuff go?"

Make a circle with your arms in front of you, as if you are hugging open space. Now sit down, holding your arms in front of you. You want your arms to encircle a bare desktop—your work space, your "hub."

Now place objects in concentric circles away from that work space—the hub—based on their *frequency of use* in relation to it. Not based on urgency, priority, or importance—those words create anxiety and stress. Your goal is progress. Frequently used items deserve the prime real estate on your desktop. Items used less frequently go at arm's reach away, in a drawer, on a shelf, or in a file. Place less used objects farther and farther away from the hub.

The principle of concentric circles creates openness because it moves items you use only occasionally out of your immediate work area. This openness makes you more efficient as you work because you'll be less distracted. You'll still have at your fingertips the things you need daily, and within arm's reach the things you need regularly. But you won't be oppressed by items you rarely use hovering over your work space.

Upright Storage

Carol is a busy manager at a large insurance company. Her handsome desk is weighed down by large piles of paper. "I know right where everything is," she insists. "Each pile represents a specific project. Still, I find I'm shuffling the piles to get things in and out. Also, I often go to the conference room to work because I feel confined at my desk."

Like most people, Carol would work more efficiently at her desk if she turned the horizontal piles into upright, vertical files. The upright storages principle improves access—tools, materials, and papers are easier to retrieve and replace when they are upright. It is easier to grab a tool from a pegboard than from a toolbox. It is easier to slide a piece of paper out of a file than out of a pile (and much easier to slide it back in!). Hooks are faster than shelves; shelves are easier than drawers. Any vertical storage option will streamline access to the tools and supplies stored there.

Using upright space also creates greater openness because it gets things off flat surfaces like counters, desks, and floors.

Simple Systems

Any system you design and use should be as simple as possible. If you set up a complicated system, you'll waste time fussing over it and maintaining it rather than using it. It will also take you longer to update when you need to adapt it to keep pace with changes in your life or responsibilities. A complicated system will frustrate you and others who need to use it. Find the most direct approach possible.

Linda is a professional presenter and author. She constantly collects stories and bits of information to use in her work. Because the writing and presenting revolve around similar topics but are not identical, she had devised an elaborate system of copying and cross-filing articles and notes in several locations. Thus a story she used in a magazine article, as background for a chapter of her last book, and in two keynote speeches and three classes could be filed in all seven of those locations, with an eighth file for a copy of the story, which she copied from a publication she receives quarterly. All this duplication took time and effort, and as a result, the file drawers were jammed so tightly that they were difficult to use, and a 30-inch pile of papers "to be filed" slouched precariously on the floor next to the file cabinets. The complicated and time-consuming system defeated itself.

By creating topic files, grouping similar or related articles and stories, and creating a short checklist or index form to add to each writing and presentation file, she could easily reference which resources she drew from when creating the piece or which she wanted to copy to hand out at the event. She eliminated the pile on the floor, generated much less paper, made citing sources simpler and more standardized, and freed up plenty of space in the file cabinet, making filing easier and files simpler to find.

Another crucial simplification is to be sure that any process or system you use is your own. Don't try to fit your work flow and lifestyle into the preprinted tabs that came with the file folders or the filing system set up by the person who had the job before you. Make the system your own, and it will be easier to use.

Scott is the office manager for a large real estate brokerage. He inherited an office full of paperwork and muddled along for four years before asking for help. Because he had never had time to assess and revamp the systems in place for ordering, invoicing, and tracking personnel files, he had created his own system on top of his predecessor's. Taking a day to FOCUS on his work flow and personal style allowed him to fully implement his own systems, integrating what he needed to from the past and eliminating the rest. He looked forward, considering the flow of paperwork into his office and anticipating what steps needed to happen to the paper before it flowed out again. He created open space by eliminating stuff (information, paper, tools, and supplies) left over from the past and no longer in use. He placed into the closest drawers and shelves those items he used most frequently and placed in more distant concentric circles things used less often. He purchased an upright file holder to contain files on his desk, and he made everything simple by eliminating duplication between the firm's paper and computer systems and streamlining the filing system so that fewer steps are required.

Five Steps to Organizing Anything

The FOCUS principles lay the foundation for solid organizing. These principles provide insight into solving any organizing challenge. But they don't tell you where to start. That's where the Five Steps to Organizing Anything come in.

1. Plan

The starting place for any organizing effort is the plan. The plan does not have to be complicated. Indeed, it should be as simple as possible. The plan is simply a statement in response to "What do you want to do with this space? This stuff? This time?" State the desired outcome succinctly: "I want to do my work at this desk." "I want to write a report with these research data." "I want to perform my job well and leave at five o'clock." Once you have a plan, it is much easier to work through the remaining steps.

Carl contacted me for help organizing his "junk room." "I just want to build floor-to-ceiling shelves and get the camping gear, hunting equipment, off-season clothes, family china, old record albums, and other junk off the floor," he said. But when we discussed his plan for the space and the stuff, it turned out he didn't really intend to camp or hunt anymore, the clothes were out of date and too small, and neither he nor his children had any interest in the old china. Instead, what he really wanted was a bathroom downstairs. So he contacted different antique and consignment shops, sold all the unwanted stuff to buy the fixtures he needed, and scheduled a week off work to remodel the room. Remember that organizing is a means to an end, not an end in itself. Think about what you really want, and then organize to achieve it.

2. Purge

If you know what you are trying to accomplish, you become more confident about what materials and information you need for that purpose. And you'll also be more confident about what you don't need. Having a good plan will help you know what you can discard.

Purging includes disposing of items altogether; donating to charity; giving to family, friends, and coworkers; and relocating objects to another part of the home or office. Any effort that removes an unneeded object is part of purging.

Joan, a self-described pack rat, told me, "I'm not good at getting rid of stuff." But with a baby on the way, she wanted to empty the nursery-to-be of her clothes and accessories. Some stuff had to go in order to fit her entire wardrobe (and her husband's) into the closet and dresser in the master bedroom. Knowing her plan—to consolidate her wardrobe—helped motivate her to the task. But knowing who could benefit from the items she no longer wore made the process of purging easier. We contacted a local charity, which not only gave Joan a receipt for her donated items but also presented her with a flyer describing the clients who would be benefiting from her donation.

Now she keeps a bag labeled for the charity at all times and makes regular visits to donate items.

3. Sort

As you purge the things you no longer need, you will naturally come across things that do support or relate to your plan. These things you will sort. Depending on the situation, you may sort by category, by use, by topic, by season, or by project. There is no right or wrong way to sort, but again, clarity in the planning process will help dictate the best sorting criteria for your circumstances.

Ellen, an artist, works in different media. Most of her tools and supplies are unique to each medium. When organizing her studio, we designated different areas for each of the different categories of craft (collage, oils, watercolors) and then sorted within each category as well. Tools and supplies that are used in all of her crafts are stored centrally, sorted by purpose (cutting, adhering, and so on).

Zach was stumped when it came to organizing his garage, a true multipurpose space where he worked on the car, repaired household items, stored sports equipment, and kept the garden tools. With use, all the materials had gravitated to the center of the space and had become mixed. His goal was to create enough room in the garage to park the car. When trying to figure out how to sort everything, we used the retail model. Zach pictured his favorite superstore and named the departments for me (Tools, Exercise, Automotive, Yard & Garden). Then we created a hub in the garage for each department and grouped all the appropriate items there. Next, we sorted within each department category, again using the retail model. So within Automotive, for example, there were such categories as filters, lubricants, and spare parts. When he was done, Zach could not only park in the garage but also move around the space comfortably and reach all the tools and supplies he needed for all his different projects.

4. Place

Once you have purged or sorted all the objects in the planned space, assess your sorted materials to determine their appropriate place. It is critical to plan, purge, and sort before attempting to place objects. Otherwise you may end up trying to fit things into the wrong-sized or -shaped container or the wrong concentric circle within the hub. For example, Joe, an avid violinist, was inspired to organize his extensive classical music collection when he saw a cool CD storage rack. But once he got home and began to sort his music into it, he discovered that it was far too small to house his collection. Frustrated, he abandoned the project and was still wading through heaps of music on the floor months later. Because he ignored the first three steps of organizing, his efforts were unsuccessful.

Beware of jumping too quickly to the placement stage. Don't try to anticipate what you'll put where or how to contain or store something until after you have carefully planned, purged, and sorted. Premature placement leads to systems that don't work. Resist buying or building any storage containers, furniture, or equipment until you have completed the first three steps.

5. Use

Finally, any new system must be used. And as you use your new system, you will modify it. That's good! Organizing is an ongoing process. You'll make some changes as you go along simply to improve the system to better fit your needs or style. And you'll make other changes because of evolving patterns in your life. One of the most common things I hear from clients is "I used to be organized, but then . . ." Life changed, but their system didn't. When life or responsibilities change, you need to change the system. Organizing is fluid, not static. Schedule time to maintain your system daily and to make larger changes periodically as necessary to support your current activities and passions.

Christopher, the president of an accounting firm, originally contacted me to help organize his files at his office. When he went into semiretirement several years later, we reorganized the files to reflect his increasing volunteer commitments. Recently, when his wife became ill, he moved his remaining files home and, now fully retired, manages the household affairs and his continued volunteer activities, as well as supervises his wife's care and medication.

Use and maintain your systems daily, and modify them when life changes.

You Can't Organize Everything All at Once

Louise came to one of my workshops and left inspired to create changes in her home. With a plan to overhaul the bedroom closet, she began to weed out clutter unrelated to dressing. Two shelves were taken up with bedding, which she determined belonged with linens rather than clothing. So she cheerfully headed to the linen closet in the hall with her arms full. But when she opened the door, sheets and towels tumbled out—knocking the linens out of her arms—and the whole mess landed in a heap on the floor. "Help!" she called.

Organizing one area inevitably leads to organizing others. But remember, things didn't get disorganized overnight, and you can't change everything at once. Organize just one area at a time. When you move things to a new and more appropriate area and find it in need of organization, schedule a time for that, but don't do it now. Go back to today's project and finish. By continuing to think in terms of use, you'll start to put things down in their logical spot even if that spot isn't organized. And as your schedule allows, you'll eventually bring greater organization to each area.

5

Organizing Space

Of the three gears—space, stuff, and time—the easiest to organize first is space. Organizing space gives an immediate visual reward for your effort and also sets the other two gears in motion. This is because as you bring greater organization to your space, you'll inevitably be handling stuff (information, paper, tools, and supplies) that you'll be putting in safe homes. You'll also be creating links to your time system (lists and calendar) for all the things you have to do. Thus by organizing space, you'll set the other gears in motion.

Creating open space is a two-step process. First, clear clutter from all flat surfaces one at a time. That includes the desktop, counter, table, shelf, windowsill, floor, and any other surfaces. After you have cleared all the flat surfaces, then you begin to delve into the inner spaces: drawers, cupboards, closets.

When organizing any space, follow the five organizing steps outlined in Chapter 4:

1. **Plan**: What do you want to do in that space?
2. **Purge**: Eliminate from the space any stuff that doesn't support the plan.
3. **Sort**: Separate the remaining stuff into categories that support the plan.
4. **Place**: Find the appropriate concentric circle for each item based on how frequently it is used in relation to the plan for that hub.
5. **Use**: Stick to the system, and modify it as needed to stay current.

To help you open your spaces and keep them open, the rest of this chapter addresses how to clear clutter, streamline paperwork, and organize the virtual desktop.

Clearing Clutter

Peggy is the owner of a large bed-and-breakfast inn. She manages seasonal and full-time permanent staff; handles all the marketing, sales, and customer relations; plans all the meals; and places all the orders. The grounds and guest areas were always neat as a pin, but the office and kitchen were in perpetual chaos. Peggy was stressed out. "I feel like I have too many balls in the air," she explained. "I don't have time to put anything away, but this clutter is getting to me." Once we had reviewed the plan, purged everything that didn't support the office and kitchen functions, created effective files and kitchen storage, and put things away, she immediately felt calmer. "I still have as much to do as ever," Peggy said, "but there is a peace about the place now that lets me work more smoothly. Taking time to put things away is almost a meditation for me now, and it feels good! Perhaps because I can focus better and because I'm not wasting time looking for things, I find I'm actually getting my work done faster even though I take time to put things away."

Clutter is anything left out on a flat surface or buried away in a storage place that is not placed there with the intention of future use or is not serving a purpose. Thus by my definition, clutter is anything that is unwanted or in the way. Getting rid of clutter gives you greater freedom of movement and thought physically, intellectually, and spiritually. This effort generates enormous positive energy. Eliminating clutter is the first step in creating open space.

Are You a Purger or a Pack Rat?

Are you one of those people who likes to get rid of things? Or are you someone who holds on to things forever? I've found that people divide almost evenly into the two camps: purgers and pack rats. Both can experience challenges with purging if it is not approached properly. And both purgers and pack rats can reap the benefits of a successful purge. A successful purge is one that leaves no regrets and generates positive energy. Both purgers and pack rats can experience the same positive emotions by following a few simple rules.

Tom doesn't like to throw things out. He is busy at home and at work and doesn't like to make the time for throwing things away. Plus he isn't quite sure which things to keep or how long he should keep them. And he has lots of interests and hobbies and collects a lot of information. This accumulated information spills into his living and working spaces. Occasionally, he gets completely fed up and heaves things. But then he often finds himself regretful and starts the cycle over again by avoiding decisions and accumulating clutter.

The way to break out of this cycle is to ensure that the organizing process is a thoughtful, deliberate one, not a frenzied, emotional one. Making decisions about information and possessions can be difficult enough without creating additional stress by operating in a whirlwind of speed and impatience. Remember, things didn't get disorganized overnight, and your goal isn't to impose order immediately but rather to methodically build sustainable habits that suit your needs for organization.

To begin the purging process, pick up the first object in front of you and ask yourself, "Do I use this?" If you answer yes, ask where you use it. That is the room or area where it belongs. And how often do you use it? That is its appropriate concentric circle in that room or area. Determining where each item goes is as simple as that. Do you use it? Yes? Where and how often? Now you know roughly where to place the object.

If the answer is "No, I don't use it," don't despair. The next questions is, "Do you *love* it?" If you shout, "*Yes!* I love it!" then the question is "*How* do you love it?" Do you want to be moved and inspired by it every day? If that's the case, put it up somewhere so that you can see it and be moved and inspired by it every day. A word of caution here: less is better. But if you can't see it, you can't be inspired by it.

A bulletin board or a refrigerator, like any space, should have a distinct purpose. Post only things that pertain to that purpose. Have a plan to purge and discard items on a regular basis so that material doesn't accumulate indefinitely and items do not become buried. Finally, respect your planned purpose—don't put things up that don't belong—and respect your plan to purge and discard items on a regular basis. Inspirations can't speak to you crumpled in the back of a drawer or buried under shopping lists on the fridge. Children's artwork, poetry, advice columns—whatever it is, make sure you can see it and be moved and inspired by it. Consider rotating items—if you leave things up indefinitely, they lose power. If you want something to be a permanent reminder, buy a frame to protect it, and hang it in a prominent location.

Some items you love, but they are not inspirations you want to see every day. Rather, they are things you want to save for posterity, as memorabilia. But ask yourself: If you're keeping them for nostalgia's sake, when do you expect to be nostalgic? There is no "later." The last thing you want to do when you are elderly and transitioning to a smaller home or a nursing facility is to wade through dozens of boxes and scrapbooks in the attic or basement. If you're saving things as memorabilia, think *now* about what you plan to do with them down the road. What are you going to do with these memories? Pass them on to grandchildren? Make collages? Write a memoir? The way you save things should be dictated by how you envision their future use as memorabilia.

Once you know how you're going to use it—annotate it. Write a simple note, date it, and add a phrase about what it means to you. You may not remember forty or fifty years from now why the object was meaningful, and your children certainly won't know unless you tell them. If it's not important enough to you now to make a quick note, it's not likely to have great meaning years from now.

If you don't use it and you don't love it but you're having a hard time getting rid of it, it is probably usable or lovable. But that doesn't mean you have to keep it! Find a local charity, pack up the car, and take it to someone else who will appreciate it. Purging to charity gives you triple returns: you free up your surroundings, you help other people, and you get a tax deduction (as long as you get a receipt for your donation).

Be Ruthless, Not Reckless

When the time comes for purging, be ruthless. If the item doesn't support and relate to your plan, purge it! But don't be reckless. Here's the difference: a ruthless process is a thoughtful, careful one in which you handle each item in turn to objectively evaluate its usefulness to you. When acting recklessly, however, you avoid thought and decision making altogether and act too quickly to acknowledge the emotions that tie you to your possessions.

It is ruthless to throw away plastic food tubs that don't have matching lids. It is reckless to throw out the china vase you adore just because it doesn't fit on the shelf. It is ruthless to discard credit card offers when you don't need a new credit card. It is reckless to discard love letters your grandparents wrote to each other.

Don't organize when you're overtired, hungry, or stressed. Prepare yourself, formulate your plan, and lay out boxes to fill with items for trash, recycling, and charity. Set aside an additional box for things that need to be moved to another part of your home or office.

Beth called me a year after her mother-in-law had passed away. "The house is like a museum," she explained. "My husband and his brother can't bear to deal with it, and it's just sitting there. We have to empty it out and sell it." Beth's mother-in-law had kept every-thing—every bill, every newspaper, every magazine, minutes from every meeting. The three-bedroom house was full—floor to ceiling, basement to attic. In several places, we could traverse the room only by turning sideways to scoot through towers of papers and boxes. Because her mother-in-law failed to differentiate the important from the mundane, she left a huge task to her children, and they were paralyzed by the effort.

At her husband's begging, Beth finally agreed to tackle the project. Because there were some gems buried in the home, they couldn't simply call an auctioneer. They felt they needed to go through everything to find the few precious items the children knew were in there: comic books from their childhood, love letters their parents wrote each other when separated by war, documentation of their grandparents' missionary work at the turn of the twentieth century in Africa. Needles in a haystack? Yes. We found all those treasures, but only by looking page by page through school records, excerpts from magazine articles, and shopping lists. "I've learned a lesson," Beth told me. "I'm going to throw out everything that doesn't have meaning and label the rest clearly so that my three kids will know what I'm leaving and why."

Why Are People Afraid to Get Rid of Things?

"If I get rid of it today, I might need it tomorrow." Well, if you don't know where it is today, you might as well have gotten rid of it yesterday! Using the FOCUS principles, you won't be reckless. You'll be anticipating your next steps, looking forward, and you won't get rid of it today if you need it tomorrow. Thinking about your next steps and the future use of an item helps you save it in a logical and accessible location. You'll simply put it in a safe home that makes sense for it, and you'll be able to find it when you need it. Note that if you throw it away today and think of it tomorrow, it's probably only because you touched it today and remembered you had it. Remembering isn't the same as needing.

"I don't know what to keep." The volume of paperwork you receive can cause paralysis, especially when much of that paperwork seems "official." What do you need to keep, and for how long? You need to keep paperwork for which you have a use, for as long as you may need to use it. Be clear what that use is, and store the paper so you can access it when that time comes. Most paper, however, has no future use. Toss it.

A conversation with your accountant and your attorney can help you develop a plan for what paperwork you need to keep. You can also refer to the general guidelines in Appendix A.

In a business setting, you need policies for the retention of paperwork. Again, if you don't know, determine who within the organization does know. Each department should develop guidelines and seek input from the company's board of directors, auditors, attorneys, or other professionals on any issues needing clarity. Everyone should know what to keep, where to keep it, and for how long.

"It was expensive." Don't hesitate to part with something simply because it was expensive. Keeping items you don't use or love costs you in terms of lost productivity and sacrificed freedom. Tally up what it is costing you to store it—by the square foot, in emotional drain, in lost opportunity for a better use of the space—and set it free. If you're holding on to something expensive, you have good options for getting rid of it. The simplest solution is to donate it to charity and take the deduction. You could instead sell or consign the item. This may put cash in your pocket but will take more time and energy than simply donating the item to charity. Finally, you can give it to someone you know who might appreciate it. You'll get neither cash nor a deduction, but you will have the satisfaction of knowing that it is in the hands of someone who really enjoys it and can use it. No

matter which option you choose, if you don't use it or love it, move it on to someone who will.

"I might lose weight and it will fit again." If you lose weight, go shopping to reward yourself! Styles change; fabrics deteriorate. Get the clothes out of your closet now so that you have room for the things you like that do fit. You're moving on with your life. And someone who is that size right now could be enjoying those items. Let them go.

"It was a gift." Just because a favorite aunt gave it to you doesn't mean you have to keep it. The love is in the giving. Someone who loved you gave you a gift. You love them? You thank them. Transaction complete. My mom told me when I was a child, "It's the thought that counts." Think good thoughts. Now get rid of all those gifts you don't use or love. I'm sure you never gave anyone a present thinking, "I love you very much, and I hope this is a burden to you for the rest of your life." The love is in the giving. Use it, love it, or give it to someone who can. You have my permission to get rid of any gift you don't use or love.

"I used to . . . Someday I might . . ." Live in the present. Don't keep things because of what you "used to" do or because of what "someday" you might do again. If you used to camp, used to knit, used to write poetry, but don't anymore, pass along all the stuff associated with

that activity. Hanging on to stuff you aren't currently using makes it harder to access the things you are using.

Don't cling to things out of "bag lady syndrome," fearing that you'll never be able to buy another pair of knitting needles or an aluminum mess kit. Don't keep a newspaper article about bee pollen because it was "interesting." There will always be people knitting, camping, and writing about health issues or any other issue or topic you choose to pursue.

If, in the future, you take up a former sport or hobby again, or if you dedicate the time to a project you've been wanting to pursue for years, I guarantee that the information, tools, and supplies for that activity will still exist. Trust that you will be able to access them, either by borrowing, buying secondhand, purchasing new, even searching the Internet. They will be there—newer, updated, and in better condition than the stuff you're hoarding in your drawers, closets, or basement.

Rather than letting the papers and equipment collect dust, deteriorate, and become outdated, get rid of them! You will benefit from discarding them, in three ways:

1. You free up space for the things you do use and love, making access easier and improving the flow of material, ideas, and energy in your surroundings.

2. You allow someone else the opportunity to pursue the sport or hobby today, in real time.

3. You get a tax deduction, the sale price, or the good feeling of sharing it with someone.

Your home or office shouldn't be a landfill. If an item is useful or lovable, somebody could be using it or loving it right now. Be honest with yourself: Think about what you want to do, and keep only what you need to do it.

Dealing with Paperwork and Mail

The general techniques for clearing clutter can be used to deal with papers, but a more specific method may help free you from the flood of papers you receive.

Karen gets home at the end of a busy day. Before she even uses the bathroom, while the dog clamors to go out and the kids whine for dinner, she gets the mail and flips through it, looking for good stuff: Any checks in here? Personal correspondence? When she comes across something that looks interesting, she opens it only to discover it is a bill or a solicitation, so she keeps flipping. After looking through the stack she slaps the whole pile on the counter, goes to the bathroom, feeds the dog, and starts dinner. When her husband comes home, he does the same thing. Sometimes even the kids shuffle through the mail. This process of peeking, shuffling, and abandoning the mail results in the "American countertop": sales flyers, bills, credit card offers, magazines and catalogs, more bills, more credit card offers, a personal letter or card . . . it's all there on your counter (or desk or dining room table) in a shuffled heap of opened and unopened envelopes, newsletters, and flyers.

RRRIPPing Through Incoming Material

RRRIPP! Isn't that a great sound? Wouldn't you just love to *RRRIPP* through your paperwork, moving quickly and decisively? The RRRIPP strategy—*refuse, recycle, refer; identify, put away, post*—is designed to protect your space (desk, counter, tabletop) from incoming papers. An abbreviated version will help you deal with the piles already on your desk.

The goal of RRRIPPing paperwork is to keep the work space open, direct papers (stuff) to safe homes based on use, and link actions to your time system. The good news is that it is compelling to keep a work space open, once you have established a system for managing papers. The bad news is that without a system, paper piles up. You've probably seen this. Paper has an unfortunate tendency to adhere to flat surfaces. And even one paper flat on a surface is the beginning of a pile. To avoid paper sticking to flat surfaces and piling up, RRRIPP through it as it enters your life. Here's how.

Refuse. To the extent that you are able, don't bring paper into your life. If you go to a meeting, a conference, a show, the supermarket, don't bring any paperwork home with you. You're not obligated to take home anything when you go somewhere. So just leave it. Don't bring it home with you unless you know what you want to do with it: unless you have a plan for how to use those data or that piece of paper is going to move you forward toward one of your goals. Don't take it home just because it is interesting or useful. Get in the habit of not putting things in your binder, your pocketbook, your briefcase, your backpack. Take it home only if you have a use for it. Refuse paperwork whenever possible.

Remember, nearly all information can be re-created. If you attend a conference and next year want to contact one of the speakers, a quick call to the conference provider can net you that phone number. So don't hoard information because "someday you might" need it. Keep only what you know you are going to use for a specific purpose.

Recycle. If you picked something up in an indecisive moment and now, upon returning to your desk or home, realize you don't have a specific use for it, recycle it immediately. Don't put it down or file it; recycle it. Similarly, if you couldn't refuse it because the postal carrier brought it but you don't have a specific use for it, recycle it immediately.

A significant portion of all mail is bulk mail, and much of that is advertisements or solicitations. That information or paper is going to come again whether you want it or not. Don't hang on to it unless you have a clear and specific use for it.

Refer. If you have paper for someone else, give or send it along immediately. Don't set the paper down; instead, put it in an envelope and send it out the door.

Now you have reached the pivotal point of the RRRIPP process: what to do if you can't refuse, recycle, or refer the paperwork.

Identify. Your first job if none of the *R*'s apply is to *identify* the action you need to take. You don't have to actually take action right now, but you absolutely have to decide what action is required of you. Be as specific as you can. Say it out loud if it helps you:

"Pay bill." Identify it using a specific verb. If the paper requires multiple actions, identify the first one. If you don't have to do anything with the paper, it is a good candidate for discard.

Even many papers that seem to need your action can be tossed. For example, if your car repair shop sends you a satisfaction survey, do you care enough to respond? It's up to you to decide. But do decide. Don't assume that you have to do everything just because someone asked. Make deliberate choices, and recycle anything that isn't part of your plan for how you want to spend your life.

Put away. Once you have identified the action you must take, you are almost done with the RRRIPP process. You continue RRRIPPing through your paperwork by putting the paper in a safe home.

Post. Finally, post a link to your time system. Posting requires that you write the action on a list and schedule time on your calendar to take the action. Simply identifying the action is not enough. To thoroughly RRRIPP through paperwork and mail, you need to be sure you keep track of the actions and schedule time for them. Organizing the "time" gear is covered further in Chapter 7.

You have now RRRIPPed though the mail without putting anything flat on your desk, table, or counter. By practicing the RRRIPP method, you protect open space, put information and paper in a safe home for future use, and track all the actions you need to pursue in your time system. This leaves you calm and focused, ready to move forward, confident that you can find what you need when it is time to pursue an activity.

RRRIPPing Through
a Cluttered Space

Lynn is the director of a nonprofit agency. She's great with people and good at details but says, "Frankly, paper seems to get lost in the shuffle." As the organization grows, Lynn needs to set up systems to handle incoming papers. "But I also need to reclaim both desks and the table in my office. Right now all three are buried in piles!"

Even if your existing spaces are cluttered, if you RRRIPP from now on, the surface will not get any worse. But you can also use the RRRIPP technique to remediate an overwhelmingly cluttered space.

With existing piles, there is nothing to *refuse* because you already have it, so begin with *recycle*. Tackle one pile at a time, and handle one piece of paper at a time. Pick it up. Recycle anything that doesn't require action from you or that you don't foresee using in the future.

If something needs to go to someone else, *refer* it to that person. Actually put it in an envelope, address it, and put it in the out box or near the door so that you can take it when you next leave the office. *Identify* the action required of you for any remaining paperwork, *put it away* in a safe home (file it), then *post* a link to your time system (lists and calendar).

RRRIPPing Through Reading Material

When RRRIPPing through your paperwork, you will inevitably identify information and paper that you want to read. Reading material requires its own set of rules.

First, acknowledge that you've probably collected far more material to read than you could possibly read, even if you had an entire week to do nothing else. Much of what you have gamely set aside to read later doesn't need to be read at all. If it did, you'd probably have read it by now. If you set it aside for an unspecified "later," you are essentially deciding not to read it. Why not just go ahead and decide not to read it now and toss it? You'll have more open space and spare yourself the guilt of having mounds of things to read.

What's the worst thing that can happen if you don't read it, anyway? Nothing. So apply the RRRIPP methodology as strictly as possible. *Refuse* any reading matter that doesn't require action on your part. That means getting off "junk" mail lists. *Recycle* material that comes if no action is required of you, even if you want to continue receiving future issues of that publication. *Refer* any literature that is of use to someone else but requires no action from you.

When you get to *identify* step, you must recognize that *read* is too vague a word to describe the action you need to take. You may want to read catalogs, trade journals, reports, financial statements, novels, and newsletters. But you probably don't read all these things for the same reasons, in the same place, or at the same time. When you identify the action, be specific. The action isn't merely to read for the sake of reading but to read for some other purpose, some further action. Identify reading material based on the action that will *follow* the act of reading. Read to amend a report you wrote, read to update your business plan, read to decide whether to give an organization more money, read for pleasure, read for inspiration. What will you do with the information after you read? Look forward, beyond the act of reading, to identify the purpose.

At this point, you can also employ the "skim and pitch" technique. If all you want is a passing familiarity with the material, don't set it aside for future reading; just take a quick glance at the headings and then toss it. By getting rid of the bulk of material, you'll have time to truly read the rest of the information.

Next, divide your reading material based on the different purposes you intend to read for, and *put them away* in different safe homes based on where you will read for that purpose. So rather than one safe home for all reading material, you need several. Once you have put the material in its safe homes, remember to *post* a link to your time system so that you can actually do the reading.

A link to your time system is the crucial step to accomplishing any action, including reading. Time systems are covered in Chapter 7. If you collect lots of reading material (because you didn't refuse, recycle, or refer it) and you don't post a link to your time system, your reading won't get done. It is crucial that you schedule time to read once you have identified a purpose for reading accumulated material.

In addition to the RRRIPP technique, with all reading material you keep, you need a system for discard. When are you going to get rid of the reading materials? For each category of reading, develop a regular system for discard so that the material doesn't accumulate. Develop a plan, and say it out loud. Say it to somebody else. "I'm

going to get rid of those *National Geographic* magazines _____."
When? Fill in the blank. It doesn't matter what the system is. It matters only that you have a system. When will you discard that category of reading material? When the next issue arrives? At the end of the year? When the bookcase is full? You decide.

And then the moment of truth arrives: it's discard day and—oh, no!—you haven't read it yet! Now you have two choices. You can let it go anyway. What's the worst thing that can happen? Probably nothing. You'll have more open space and less guilt. Or you can set aside more time to read. Make appointments with yourself to read—actually write them on your calendar. Be specific. Actively choose to read rather than do whatever else you had planned for your time. If you want to get more reading done, you'll have to set aside more time for reading and less time for something else.

Janet gets a lot of reading material. She works from home as a fundraising consultant, so the daily mail includes personal as well as professional information. When RRRIPPing through the day's influx, she identifies nine categories of reading material. Janet's process demonstrates how all the different reading material goes to different places based on its use:

- Read to improve professional skills (*Fundraising Today*).
  Put in purse to scan when waiting to pick up boys from

hockey practice; toss when finished skimming or when next
week's issue arrives.

- Read to revise for clients (draft paperwork prepared by
  client for her review). Put in client's file in desk and write
  on calendar to spend two-hour block tomorrow morning.
  Then put in client's file after faxing changes to client.
  Discard when client sends copy of final document with
  changes.

- Read to properly fill out proposal (invitation to bid on a
  large new client project). Create file for potential client and
  put one-hour block on calendar for Friday. After preparing
  bid, put in "bids pending" folder. Discard after bid award
  date if not awarded the project. If awarded bid, move to a
  client folder until completion of project.

- Read for dates of programs and events (local hiking club
  newsletter). Skim quickly right now and note all events in
  pencil on calendar; circle ones she wants to go to and put
  at kitchen table so boys can decide which ones they might
  want to attend.

- Read to buy (clothing catalog). Put by TV to flip through
  during commercials, circle items she wants, and put in

online folder for when she is next surfing the Web. Throw out once items have been ordered.

- Read for pleasure (popular magazines). Put by bed to leaf through before falling asleep. Toss all on last recycling day of the month.

- Read for recipes (cooking magazines). Place by kitchen table to flip through over Sunday breakfast while planning meals for the week.

- Refer (*Sports Illustrated*). Goes in the boys' bathroom upstairs until the basket by the toilet gets full; then recycle all of them.

- Refer (*National Geographic*). Goes on the coffee table in the living room for everyone to look at; when next issue arrives, it goes on bookshelf until end of year, when family recycles entire year's worth.

Having a pile that you never read isn't much different from recycling it in the first place, except that it feels better to actually decide up front to toss things you'll never read. Take a hard look at the reading material you've accumulated at home and at work. For a fresh start, purge all of it and start today RRRIPPing reading material as it comes in the door. If all you need is permission to toss all the old stuff out and start over, you have mine. If that feels a little reckless to you, RRRIPP through the existing pile, reducing it as much as you can and dividing the reading material based on use. Put each different type of reading in its safe home, and post time to read in your time system. Then ruthlessly RRRIPP all incoming material.

The Law of In-Boxes

Did you know that it is a federal offense to put anything in your mailbox except outgoing mail? You can't use your mailbox as a storage receptacle for miscellaneous items, for bills you haven't paid yet, or for newspaper articles that tick you off. The U.S. Postal Service has strict rules: the mailbox exists for incoming and outgoing mail, period.

If you have an in-box at work, treat it like a federal mailbox: other people put things in it, and you take things out. Your job is to keep the paper flowing. If you fail to respect this system, people will lose confidence in your in-box as a method for getting things to you, and they'll start to violate your open space by putting paperwork on your chair or your keyboard in an effort to ensure your attention. Respect the law of in-boxes: They put it in, you take it out, and if you don't recycle or refer it, you identify the action you're going to take, then put it in a safe home and post a note on a list in your calendar.

Virtual Desktop

By applying the same methodical approach to your computer, you'll be able to organize your virtual desktop as well as your tangible one.

When you turn your computer on, the desktop should not be cluttered with unused icons. Create open space so you don't have to weed through unnecessary programs or files to find what you need. Use the concentric circles principle to determine which program icons deserve to be in plain view. Delete or hide the others so they are not in your way.

When it comes to storing documents on your computer, you'll need more than one folder titled "My Documents." Imagine a four-drawer file cabinet stuffed full of all the documents ever created since you began your job, with no category groupings, no folders, and no headings, just individual documents. That's the physical example of putting all your documents in the "My Documents" folder. Sure, you can sort by document title or date, but it's still overwhelming.

The placement of documents on your computer should more or less mirror the placement of documents in your actual file drawers. Create file folders on your computer that relate to the broad categories of the projects you're pursuing. Within each folder, you'll probably need a number of subfolders. In some cases, it may be helpful to group folders chronologically by month, quarter, or year to make it easier to find, sort, and discard information. Once you have created appropriate folders, be sure that you save documents to them, not simply to the desktop or to the "My Documents" general heading.

If you generate a lot of files, establish naming conventions for the different types of files you create to make it easier to search for them. For example, begin all documents related to clients with a client name or code, all letters with the designation LTR, all contracts with a CON, and so on. When creating naming conventions, use a system or code that is simple and straightforward so you that don't confuse yourself or avoid using it.

Even in the virtual world, don't mindlessly accumulate. Keep only what you are going to use. Then set up a regular schedule for reviewing what you have where and purging what is no longer needed.

Note, however, that while I generally recommend permanently deleting files you have no future use for, you can, for a relatively modest cost, store an entire life's worth of work on a 120-gigabyte hard disk with plenty of room to spare. Archiving electronic data is inexpensive and easy. And unlike paper, it takes up practically no physical space. Thus armed with a good plan for what you might need in the future, you can easily archive it.

Both on your computer and on your backup drive, create sufficient folders and subfolders so that you can easily file documents in a logical way. Though it is possible to search the entire drive, you can make your job easier and faster by planning where files belong and saving them to their appropriate folders. This will prevent clutter in your directories.

Patrick is a computer programmer with lots and lots of data. Here's how he solved the problem on his computer. "I open up space in my directory by moving documents on a regular basis into a quarterly folder (such as 'Documents-2003-Q1'), which then goes into a folder called 'Documents,' which is itself in a folder called 'Archives.' Now all I 'see' at the top level is 'Archives'—which can contain a practically infinite amount of data. But I still have lots of 'open space' in my working directory. By building a decent filing system of folders in the directory, I can deal with massive e-mail and data loads. All

I have to do is push stuff I don't need down farther in the directory tree so that it's not in my way."

Finally, be sure you have a regular plan to back up needed data. Establish a system for backup and discard so that you know when to get rid of things and can ensure the safety of the things you don't want to delete. It doesn't matter what your policy or schedule is. What matters is that you have one to protect yourself in case of a computer malfunction. Make this maintenance part of a regular routine.

With a little planning and regular discipline, your virtual desktop will be free of clutter and you'll be functioning efficiently.

RRRIDding Yourself of E-Mail

Today the volume of e-mail you receive may dwarf daily paper mail. Although e-mail can be an effective way to communicate, e-mail overload can seriously diminish your productivity.

First, recognize that e-mail is not a spice—don't pepper your day with it. If the postal carrier came to your house twenty, fifty, or a hundred times a day, you'd be feeling pretty harassed. So why allow e-mail to pop up at you all day long, interrupting your work?

Take charge of your e-mail. Decide when in the day you are going to deal with it. And then, like paper mail, resolve to not read any e-mail until you commit to dealing with all of it. Just as with paper mail, resist the temptation to look for the good stuff, leaping over the less exciting notes. Work methodically through each message with a goal of RRRIDing yourself of the message: *refuse, recycle* (or delete), *refer, identify, do.*

Mary attended one of my seminars. A month later, I received an e-mail from her: "Painstakingly," she wrote, "I have removed every nonessential document from my inbox (all 2,600 messages—no, I'm not kidding or exaggerating!) At the moment it is completely empty." Eight months later, she reported that although she still struggles with the discipline needed to RRRID herself of e-mail on a daily basis, she is feeling more efficient and more confident that her follow up is thorough.

RRRIDing yourself of e-mail is the virtual corollary to RRRIPPing through paperwork and mail. The purpose is the same: to create open space and to prevent that open space from becoming cluttered, while at the same time directing information and paper to safe homes and ensuring that you take action. Remember, mailboxes are meant to be trampolines, not parking lots. Don't let anything languish in your in-box. Other people put it there; your job is to take it out and keep it going. Your in-box—be it tangible or virtual—is not a place to store anything. It is for incoming mail only.

In the context of e-mail, *refuse* means to get off all the lists you possibly can. Choose not to receive any information, updates, or newsletters that don't help you toward your goals. Ask to be deleted from FYI communications. As much as possible, only receive information you have to act on.

Recycle (or delete) any e-mail that doesn't require action on your part but isn't something you can prevent from coming in the future. You can easily skim and pitch many e-mails. Quickly read each e-mail and delete it before moving on to the next one.

As with paper mail, if the information is more suited to someone else, *refer* it to the person right away. Don't leave in your in-box. Forward it and delete it from your in-box.

Finally, some e-mail is directly relevant to your work and requires some action on your part. Immediately *identify* the action, and then *do* it.

Unlike receiving paper mail, which is an exercise in sorting, receiving e-mail is an action in itself. Most e-mail that requires an action requires a response. So *do* it: respond, and then delete the message. If you don't have enough time to respond when you receive your e-mail, you are probably receiving e-mail too often and not allowing enough time to RRRID yourself of it all at each sitting. You should get your e-mail a limited number of times each day and schedule enough time to actually process it during that period. Some messages may be useful to keep over time. If so, get the message out of your in-box and into an appropriately labeled project or subject file so that your in-box remains empty, ready to receive incoming mail.

If you are unable to respond because you have to gather additional information outside of your e-mail session, make a note in your time system regarding what you have to do. If you routinely process e-mail thoroughly enough that there remain only a few messages that require a response after having gathered additional data, you might bend the rule and leave them in the inbox for your next session. Otherwise, create a folder for messages requiring your response following receipt of additional information from another source.

Patrick, the computer programmer, has this to say about storing e-mail: "I get about seventy-five to one hundred e-mails a day, of which probably half are pure spam (and get deleted instantly), half the rest are mass mailings (which might get skimmed and deleted but most likely just get deleted); the rest require actual attention (this chunk triples when my team is working on a problem). I send ten to thirty a day. I keep *all* of the stuff that survives the first delete. But there's *nothing* in the inbox; I RRRID ruthlessly, and my filing system is just 'In-2003-Q1' and 'Out-2003-Q1.' I've got little chunks like that back to 1995, and I can search *all* of it."

Be sure you allow enough time when you process e-mail to respond to prior e-mails, whether they stay in your in-box or in another folder. More than half a dozen e-mails in your in-box suggests you are not thoroughly RRRIDing yourself of them, which means you need to get off more lists, recycle (delete) more ruthlessly, or allocate more time during the day to process e-mail. Be realistic about how long it takes. Remember the law of in-boxes: other people put things in; you take them out and act on them to keep them moving. Don't leave messages in your in-box. They make it harder to keep track of actions you need to take and harder to focus on those actions when you pursue them.

Finally, help others out when you send e-mail. Use the subject line as an action line. When you send someone an e-mail, state in the subject line what action you want the person to take, and ask people who send you e-mail to do the same. This technique helps when passing along tangible papers too. Always let the recipient know what action you expect so that he or she doesn't wonder what to do with the papers. Never send someone an e-mail (or a communication of any sort) without knowing clearly what you expect the recipient to do with the information. Otherwise, you aren't communicating—you're dumping.

Quickly RRRID yourself of e-mail by *refusing, recycling, referring, identifying* the action or response, and *doing* it. By diligently applying the RRRID principles, you'll have an empty e-mail box and amaze your friends and coworkers with how much you accomplish in a timely fashion.

Keeping the Gears Turning

I guarantee you that if you have safe homes for your stuff and you use a time system to record actions you have to take, you will not lose things and you will not miss deadlines. Unfortunately, many people will not do this. It takes effort. But once you create an open space, you will be motivated to keep it that way. That's why you should start organizing with the space gear: organize surfaces first.

Organizing the space gear is an immediate and visually rewarding experience. Once you have created open space on your surfaces, you'll want to keep them clutter- and pile-free—both because it looks good and because it works so well. Organized space keeps your stuff and time gears moving as well. Each time you put something away in a safe home and link the action to your time system, you start those gears turning.

6

Organizing Stuff

So where are the safe homes for stuff? Stuff includes information, paper, tools, and supplies. The safe home for tools and supplies is storage. The safe home for information and paper is a specific type of storage called files.

Use the forward thinking principle when finding a safe home for anything (information, paper, tools, or supplies). Ask yourself how you will next use the item. Where? And how often? These questions will help you determine the hub, or main area, where it belongs, and within that hub, the concentric circle—how close to the center of the hub—it belongs.

Maximizing Storage

The less you have, the easier it is to store and access. Although you may think you have inadequate storage, the problem is more likely that you have too much stuff. The top three ways to maximize storage are to purge regularly, to purge more often, and to purge more ruthlessly.

The growth of the off-site storage industry has ballooned in the past decade. Why? Because people are accumulating more stuff than they can possibly use. Filling up storage bins is the ultimate in the "I used to" and "Someday I might" mentality. It costs you money and wraps a ball and chain around your ankles. If you find yourself renting off-site storage for any reason other than temporary short-term transitions, it is a red flag that it is time to simplify and downsize.

Resist the urge to purchase when you can rent or borrow. Cure yourself of the compulsion to acquire and cling. Get in the habit of purging on a daily basis. Force yourself to decide what you're going to do with anything that comes into your life. Once you've identified the action, you can put it in its safe home—the hub where you're going to use it and the concentric circle based on how often you're going to use it. If you aren't going to do anything with it, get rid of it. Keep a charity box right by the door or near recycling, and put something in it every day.

Beyond regular and vigorous purging, storage can best be maximized by following the Five Steps to Organizing Anything discussed in Chapter 4: *plan, purge, sort, place, use.* Never lose sight of the plan—what are you trying to accomplish in that space. Then purge and sort.

Placement is the most critical stage of maximizing storage. Remember not to get ahead of yourself. Before you begin placement, really study the space, remembering your plan. Think strategically about the space and be creative—find a storage solution that suits your work patterns and lifestyle. Give yourself time to consider your needs, and brainstorm several options.

Sarah, at 8 years old, had a passion for Barbies. Even after discarding dismembered or unloved ones, she still had thirty-nine. She had been keeping them in a bin, but they were hard to find and got tangled. When I asked her to think creatively about how she might be able to get the ones she wanted easily but still see them all without piling them on the windowsill or the floor, she decided to hang a rope from the ceiling, attach tube socks to it with clothespins, and stick each Barbie in its own tube sock. She had the ones she played with all the time down low and the ones she just liked to look at up high.

Her mother was appalled. But Sarah was delighted because for the first time ever, she could see her Barbies, reach them, and put them away easily. This convinced her mother that the best system is the one that works.

Think about how frequently you use items in each category, and look at the space to determine how close to you things should be. Be alert to opportunities to take advantage of upright space. Then measure—literally, with a tape measure—before you build or shop for shelves, bins, file drawers, or storage units. Before you shop, know exactly how much room you have in any given space (make a map and note the dimensions of the space), and know how much room you need (linear or square feet) for storage in each category. Allow room for growth to prevent crowding.

Once you find the right containers and get things put away, label where everything goes. A labeled system is easier for you to maintain and increases the likelihood that others will help you maintain the system.

Tessa was eight months pregnant with her second child when she called me, having recognized that her kitchen was out of control. We tamed the piles of paper, established an office nook, and re-organized all the cupboards to streamline access so that Tessa could find what she needed quickly and easily after the baby was born. Then we labeled all the shelves. "No one could believe it, but this was the best prebaby preparation I did," she told me a year later. "Anytime anyone offered to help after the baby was born, I sent them to the kitchen. Neighbors, in-laws, even my husband could easily prepare a meal or clean up, and things got put away in the right places. Now my older child is starting to learn to read the labels, and he likes to help put things away, too!"

Finally, use the system. Don't expect it to run itself. Make changes as necessary so that your systems support your life.

Filing

The Five Steps to Organizing Anything, with an emphasis on purging, purging, and more purging, will improve your filing storage just as it does any storage challenge. But there are more tips and tricks to organizing papers.

The safe home for paper stuff is a file of some sort. Before you panic, let me assure you that filing doesn't have to be a painful experience. Most people who are demoralized or terrified by files have had negative experiences with them for one (or several) of these reasons:

- They jammed the gears, using stuff (files or paper) as a time management system.

- They were using files set up by or dictated by someone else.

- The filing system lacked a plan for the information and paper's use.

A filing system is nothing more than a safe home for the paper you are going to use. And even though a filing system does not have to be a file drawer, it must be an upright system—a file rather than a pile—because access is easier when things are upright. It is easier to slide a paper in and out of an upright file than in and out of a horizontal pile. To get a piece of paper out of a pile, you have to shimmy it out, being careful not to create an avalanche of paper into the next pile. And even if you get it out successfully, you still face the challenge of putting it back in the same place. This feat requires shuffling the pile. If you simply turn the piles on end so that they become vertical files, it will be easier and faster to slip things in and out of them.

I recommend hanging files that slide in drawers, but a "file" can be any upright system for storing papers. You can store papers upright in cubbyholes, baskets, or bins if you prefer the way they look and feel. Turning piles into upright files also frees up desk space, giving you the openness you need to concentrate on your work.

Visualize your files sorted into four categories: action, project, resource, and archive.

Action Files

Action files are those you are in and out of every day. They never get fat. Action files are not a permanent home for anything. They represent tedious or administrative actions you need to do every day. The tabs on these files are labeled with action verbs: PAY bills, ENTER data, BROWSE online, CALL, WRITE, and so on. Action files are the closest link between your stuff (information and paper) and your time. They provide a place to corral information and paper or paper associated with frequent actions. The actions themselves (call, write, enter, and so on) should be noted in your time system.

The action file doesn't tell you to perform the action; the time system does that. The action file is simply a place to store information and paper until you need it. Because you are in and out of them daily, action files deserve the closest proximity to your work space. You may even keep them on your desktop—upright, of course—in a file holder.

Susan is a sales manager for a ski accessory manufacturer. When she is on the road, she receives a huge volume of voice mail, and she also receives "inquiry order forms" from prospects. To make her callbacks most efficiently, she asks callers in her voice mail message to leave their name, phone number (twice), reason for the call, and when they can be reached. When she retrieves her messages, she records the data consistently with all the message notes in the same format, and she has learned to corral them into an action folder on her desk together with the inquiry order forms that require a callback. Keeping the call information together and in a designated location has ended hours of searching for sticky notes and slips of paper with messages and phone numbers.

Project Files

Slightly farther away, in the next concentric circle, you place your project files. Project files represent the work you do and the information and paper that you generate. These are files that you're in and out of for the duration of the relationship or the project. They often get quite large and may need to be divided into segments. Project files are generally kept in the file drawers of the desk or within easy reach of the desk. Purge them at the end of the project or relationship.

Where does a paper go if it is part of a project but requires action? Information should always go in its most permanent safe home. So, if information has a permanent home in a project file, it always lives with the project file. If you have to take an action regarding that project, make a note in your time system or in your action file or in both places. For example, let's say you have to call a contractor about a building construction project, and you've got some drawings that you want to discuss with him. The drawings live in the building project file. A note to call the contractor—"call Joe re: drawings"—goes in the call file or on the call list. Use the action files as a place to corral papers that relate to a regular action but will be discarded once the action is completed.

Here's another example: if you get a flyer about going to an organizing workshop and you have to call to find out if you can afford it and if there's space, it goes in your call folder. Then you call. You get in. You pitch the flyer, write the details of time and place on your calendar, and you're done. Or if you call and learn that there's no space, you simply pitch the flyer. Information only goes in the call file until the call is made, and then it moves to another location. Sometimes, after you make the call, you throw it out. Sometimes, after you make a call, you end up creating a project file. Nothing lives permanently in an action file. It is only there until the action is completed, and then it goes away or becomes part of a larger file. For instance, if you are returning a call to a prospect who inquired about your services, and as a result of the call, a consultation is set up, the prospect has now become a client, and so you set up a project file.

Resource Files

What is probably clogging your file drawers is information that seemed interesting but that—let's be honest—you'll never reach for again.

Linda is very interested in health. She has files called "Health," "Alternative Health," "Medical Reference," "Supplements," "Vitamins," "Bee Pollen," and on and on. Not surprisingly, she often can't decide where to file an article, nor can she reliably find an article she has clipped, because there are too many likely possibilities for it.

When I suggested that she could recycle every single one of

those files, Linda balked at first. But when we examined the articles one by one, she agreed that she didn't actually have a plan for how she would use the information and that it could easily be re-created in several ways if she did decide to use it. Any topic that interests you is undoubtedly of interest to others, and information on it will continue to be generated, updated, and circulated. If you choose to pursue it later, you can get the information again—in a more current version—through traditional sources or via the Internet.

Effective resource files support and relate to what you do, but they are not created by you. Since they are created by some other source, they are usually easy to re-create, because someone else generated them and could do so again.

Resource files belong in the third concentric circle—usually a file drawer near or behind your desk.

Archives

With archives, as with all papers, look forward: How will you use this in the future? Archives belong in the farthest concentric circle, in a storage area out of your immediate work space. There are only two types of archives: historical (for memorabilia) and fiscal (for tax matters).

Regarding memorabilia, keep only what truly speaks to you. Annotate it. Keep it in a way that will preserve it from mold, moisture, and vermin. In certain circumstances, you may want to maintain a slim file to document your business or professional history, but don't get carried away. This type of memorabilia is often useless to future generations, so be sure that what you keep will be meaningful and useful. Beware of simply hoarding old projects, calling them "archives." If you have a use for old projects—to inform a future project or to serve as a template, for example—store them in a way that will allow easy access when you need it. But don't simply keep all your old work as an "archive." Old projects shouldn't be archived unless they have historical value.

The second type of archive is the paperwork saved for tax purposes. A conversation with your accountant and your attorney can help you develop a plan for what paperwork you need to keep. But be realistic—Uncle Sam doesn't need the instruction booklets! Don't fall into the trap of keeping more than you need.

Note that placement of files is based on use, not urgency or priority or importance. Action files corral information related to your daily repetitive tasks and are kept close at hand because you use them frequently each day. Project files permanently house paperwork related to your core work and creative responsibilities and should be within easy reach. Resource files hold information and paper you use that supports and relates to what you do, but that was created by someone else. Because you use them less often than the files representing your own work—your project files—they belong slightly farther away from your work space. And farthest away from your work area store archives containing tax-related paperwork (for seven years) and memorabilia (until you're ready to pass it on).

Bill is a supervisor at a social service agency. He's involved in several large planning projects. One involves affordable housing. When his secretary delivers his mail, he receives a thick envelope of paper with several very different pieces in it about that project. One is a new regulation he needs to review and discuss with his housing manager. One is a final contract from the organization's attorney that he needs to sign, another is a bill from the attorney, and yet another is a flyer about upcoming training sessions on the new regulations. Bill knows he needs to talk to the builder working on one of their apartment units to be sure he is up to speed on this new regulation. Lots of actions, lots of paper—where does it all go? The answers are based on Bill's actions: What does he have to do?

First, Bill signs the contract, puts it in an envelope, and puts it in his out-box. He then approves the bill and puts it in his out-box for the accounting department. Next, he knows he isn't going to attend the training sessions, so he puts that and the regulations in his out box to his housing manager with a note: "Please review these regulations prior to our meeting Friday to highlight any changes relevant to our projects. Choose a training session for you and the housing staff to attend, and sign up. Thanks!" Finally, he makes a note in his "Builder" file to check with the builder at their next regular meeting to be sure he has the regulation information he needs. In this way, Bill has kept his desk clear, sent all the information on its way, and created links to events and activities scheduled on his calendar to ensure follow up. Everything is kept in motion.

The fable of the tortoise and the hare illustrates the power of deliberate, planned progress. The one who wins the race is the tortoise, who keeps moving steadily along, step by step. We all want to get things done. To be most effective, establish systems that allow you to proceed at a steady pace. Rushing in a frenzy from one emergency to another only causes anxiety, exhaustion, and burnout. If you advance steadily, you'll get there—surely, calmly, and probably first.

As an added bonus, once you get in the habit of proceeding methodically, it will be easier to keep track of what is truly time-sensitive.

By having open space and safe homes and all your actions linked to your time system, you can stay on top of deadlines, focus on one task at a time, and keep track of papers without fear. If your action files are thin enough and you're in and out of them every day, it will be immediately clear to you, when you look in that file first thing in the morning, what you have to do right away. And that will shape your plan for the day. Again, keeping the gears separate allows them to work together to move you forward.

Filing Dos and Don'ts

How do you keep filing from getting out of hand? Never lose sight of the fact that you are filing information so that you can find it again. Don't file to entomb papers. File based on your plan for future use. Then follow these simple tips to keep the files manageable:

- Do file. Don't pile.

- Do create your own system. Don't try to use the system you inherited or use the tabs that came with the folders.

- Do put files in upright file holders or file drawers. Don't stack them on every available flat surface.

- Do put each piece of paper neatly into the file, with all the papers facing the same way. Don't jam papers in every which way or allow them to get folded and dog-eared.

- Do staple papers together if they need to stay together. Don't use paper clips—they grab things you don't want them to grab.

- Do purge regularly. Don't set up a system and stuff it until it explodes.

- Do label your files and create an index to tape to the front of the drawer. But don't make the system complicated. Keep it as simple as possible.

- Do align folder tabs randomly or line them all up on one side or the other except when you want to set off a specific file or group of files. Don't attempt to stagger folders perfectly—your system will only be thwarted when you add or delete a file.

- Do use color if it is meaningful. Don't get carried away. A rainbow effect is distracting.

- Do keep lots of manila folders on hand. Don't buy lots of different-colored folders. Colored folders are more expensive, and you will inevitably run out of the color you want at a crucial moment. Keep it simple by using only manila folders and writing on the tab (you can use colored markers if you want to, or else draw a line across the top of the tab in a color). Then you'll always have folders on hand, and you can easily reuse the manila folders by putting a label over the tab.

Filing can be easy if you keep it simple, current, and personal.

Using Your Files

In the first few weeks with your new system, make it especially easy on yourself by creating a "cheat sheet," a line-by-line index of every file in every drawer. Tape this to the front of each drawer. Chant the cheat sheet every time you file. It sounds silly, and it's going to make you laugh, but every time you file, which will be many times each day, chant your index out loud before sliding that paper into its folder. Here's what this does for you: First, it familiarizes you with the categories and file names you created. This increases the speed and confidence with which you retrieve and replace files. Second, as you hear yourself, you'll rename and move files to better reflect your needs and interests. And finally, you'll prevent duplication and embed consistency. You'll never again end up with files called "Car Insurance," "Insurance—Car," "Toyota," and "Auto." You'll develop regular patterns for filing protocols that make sense to you, and you'll be able to stick to them.

There should never be a file pile. Put paper in safe homes by RRRIPPing through it as it enters your life. A file pile isn't a safe home because you won't be able to find what you need when you need it. Send it all the way to where it needs to go.

Now that you've invested the time to create a great new file system, use it every single time you have something to be filed. If your system is too complicated or awkward to allow quick and easy filing throughout the day, the system needs to be simplified to improve access. If it's awkward or difficult, it will be self-defeating.

There's no right or wrong way to file. The right way is your way. Set up your system, use the system, and change it as necessary to best suit your needs.

Tips for Visual Thinkers

If you're a visual thinker, the last thing you want is to have all your paperwork visible. Be especially careful that the only thing out is the one thing you want to be focusing on right now.

"But," you wail, "if I don't leave it out, I'll forget to do it!" Don't jam your gears. Stuff is not a time-management tool. If you leave your stuff out to remind you to do things, you'll only end up with lots of stuff out, creating a distracting environment. If you haven't been able to put things away because you can't trust your calendar, fix that—don't just create an additional problem by leaving things out in your way.

7

Organizing Time

The concept of time management is grossly misunderstood. At time management seminars, participants are often less interested in changing lifestyles and work patterns to maximize productivity than in discovering a "magic" system or, even less realistically, extra time. "Time management" is an oxymoron. Individuals can no more manage time than they can command the sun to rise and set. Time is inelastic. Everyone gets the same amount of time every day. Some people, however, *use* their time more effectively than others. Your goal, then, is not to have more time but to choose consciously how you allocate the time you have.

By learning the Five Steps to Organizing Anything, applying them to your space and your stuff, and creating a link to your time system, you will inevitably become much more effective in your use of time. There is no magic to it. It is a simple exercise in the consistent application of a skill. Organizing time involves employing systems—in this case, lists and a calendar—to effectively allocate your time to reach your objectives.

It is easier to organize the time gear last because the results with space and stuff are much more visible, more tangibly rewarding, and therefore more compelling to maintain. This gives you confidence to apply the Five Steps to the way you manage your time, knowing that you'll achieve the same rewarding results.

Furthermore, no matter how effectively you plan and execute your day, your carefully laid plans will be wasted if you have no clear space to work or if you can't find things. For you to get done what you set out to do, you must have open space to work and safe homes for your stuff.

Managing Lists

Lists are a useful way to catalog thoughts and ideas. You can use lists to record people invited to a party, movies recommended to you, and groceries to buy. The purpose of a list within the time gear is to keep track of activities you want to pursue. Your daily list need not include every item you ever hope to accomplish; rather it should simply include the steps you need to take in the near term.

Lists can take many forms: electronic, paper, sticky notes, pages in calendar—whatever works for you. They should be separated into headings or categories, though the headings will differ for each person. Common action headings include verbs such as *call, pay, write, e-mail, browse, enter data, report,* and *develop.* Lists can also be kept by project or topic or even by location of activity or task. Lists provide more detail than the calendar, which usually just indicates the action scheduled for a period of time. But lists should not include the level of detail that can be found in an action or project folder.

Yes, you have to rewrite and update your list from time to time. But this process prompts you to reprioritize and make choices. If you find you are recopying whole pages frequently, it is a sign that you're trying to do way too much or keeping too much detail on your list. The list should be brief, recording what you have to do. Details or additional paperwork belong in an action or project folder.

The "Right" Calendar

Here's what's important about calendars: have one. Everybody should have one calendar and only one. Not one for work and one for home, but one you like and keep with you at all times so that you don't overbook or double-book yourself. If you work as part of a team or live with others in a family setting, it is helpful to have a team or family calendar—a central place where major commitments, deadlines, and group gatherings are noted. But you should upload and download information from your calendar to the central one and vice versa. Your calendar is unique to you. Keep it with you at all times, and record all of your commitments in it.

There is no "right" kind of calendar. Each calendar is as good as the person who chooses it and uses it. What you need to do is find a calendar you like well enough to actually use. Before shopping, think about your personal preferences.

Both paper and electronic calendars have unique features. Paper calendars are generally less expensive, simple to use, and not subject to loss of battery power. A more familiar and comfortable choice for many people, paper calendars work perfectly well for millions of users.

Electronic calendars have the benefit of storing huge quantities of data, offer search capability, prevent you from having to enter repeating events, provide multiple views (day, week, month) without entering the data multiple times, allow you to share your schedule with others, come with games and many fun extra functions, provide password protection for data, and last but not least, give you a means to back up your entire calendar to your desktop computer, protecting the data in case of theft, loss, or power malfunction.

Both kinds of calendars can be accessorized with note pads, places for business cards, and other useful amenities, depending on the style of cover or notebook you purchase to hold the calendar.

Choosing a calendar really comes down to personal preference. If you are comfortable with technology, electronic calendars provide excellent functions. If your work requires you to have lots of contact information at your fingertips or if you like to see day, month, and year at a glance without entering data multiple times, or if you need to share your calendar with several members of a team, an electronic calendar is probably the right choice. I also recommend electronic calendars for people with busy schedules who like a lot of detail in their calendars but who have big, sloppy handwriting. Paper calendars are fine for people who enjoy the feel and experience of paper and writing and who don't need huge volumes of data at their fingertips when scheduling time.

Buy what you need and are comfortable with, and don't buy more. Your system should be as simple as possible to help you schedule your projects. The bottom line is that whatever you choose, you have to use. And if you've made a choice that doesn't seem like a good fit, you need to experiment with another choice until you find a style and system that suit you. Remember to examine what you are trying to accomplish, and keep the method for accomplishing it as simple as it can possibly be.

Two Components of the Time Gear: Lists and Calendar

When you're organizing your space and stuff, you continually create links to the time system for all the things you have to do. These links are generally notations on a list or series of lists. As you note each action, you'll begin to see repetition of tasks or activities. Categorize each list or section of a list by these repeated actions. Then, when you are ready to organize your time, analyze the lists and build a structure on your calendar to ensure that each action heading (each list or section of the list) has a block of time on your calendar.

Let's look more closely at how to create a structure using these two elements of the time gear: lists and calendar. Use lists to collect the activities you intend to pursue and group the action into headings. Use your calendar to record all your commitments to yourself and to others. Note that your commitments include more than just your appointments with other people. If you use your calendar only to schedule appointments, you'll probably get to most of them. But you may find yourself frustrated with your productivity outside of meetings. Neither lists nor a calendar is sufficient independently. For the time gear to function, you must engage both of these components. Collect the actions on a list, and schedule the actions on your calendar.

If something isn't on your calendar, it isn't likely to get done. Short of going to the bathroom, which everyone does and no one writes down, if you want to get something done, it had better be written down. You may balk when I suggest this, claiming, "If I put everything I had to do on my calendar, I'd need a book the size of the Bible." If that is the case, you're trying to do too much. How can you possibly expect to get it all done if you can't even write it all down? Don't try to do more than your week will allow. Give yourself a break.

To organize the time gear, apply the Five Steps to Organizing Anything, discussed in Chapter 4. First, *plan.* The plan for your time doesn't have to be complicated, but think in the broadest way about what you want to do: succeed at work? spend time with family?

Armed with a plan for your time, you can now *purge* anything that doesn't support your plan. If it doesn't connect to your plan and your goals, take it off the list. What's the worst thing that can happen if you don't do it? Probably nothing. This makes it easier to say no because you can weigh any action against your plan—does the prospective activity support your desire to be with loved ones? pursue your passions? If not, say no. If it does, your next step is to *sort.*

All activities you have to do fall into general categories. If you list your actions beginning with a verb, you'll discover you have lots of repetition—for example, lots of *call* or *meet with* or *drive to* or *shop for*. Group these similar tasks together using the verb as a heading.

Now *place* each heading on your calendar in a given block of time. Seriously. Decide what time or times each day you will make calls, respond to e-mail, be available for meetings, study with your children, and so on. Whatever you've decided to do, make time for it on your calendar. As you design this template, keep your personal rhythms in mind. If you're sharper in the morning, schedule your thinking projects then, and leave the afternoons open for meetings, phone calls, and smaller projects that require less concentration. After you have placed each heading, step back and look at the shape you have created for your day. Consider your goals for work and for home, and make changes to this template to accommodate the way you want to spend your time.

Remember Susan, the sales manager with dozens of calls to return? She found that by scheduling callbacks on her calendar three times daily, she was able to steadily work her way through calls accumulated in her action file labeled "Calls." She also let people know what times of day she preferred to receive calls, diminishing the number of calls she received during the times she scheduled for quiet, uninterrupted work. She has also found it useful to have one of her scheduled callback times to be at odd hours so that she can simply leave a message, avoiding unnecessary chitchat.

Having a template blocking time for scheduled tasks gives your day structure and allows you to visually compartmentalize all the tasks and projects you seek to fit into the day. This allows you to recognize when you have taken on an unrealistic load, giving you the opportunity to make choices about what to say no to. It also gives you a format to rearrange if activities don't go as planned. By seeing your day, week, and month blocked out with tasks, you can clearly recognize what you gave up when you chose to deviate from your plan. *Using* the system doesn't mean slavishly adhering to your schedule. It means recognizing that there is a schedule and making conscious choices to change it without losing sight of your intentions.

The Colored Sticky Note Exercise

This exercise illustrates how time blocking helps you keep track of your time. Assemble a large collection of sticky notes in different colors. After sorting all your activities into categories and giving each category a heading, assign each heading a color of sticky note. As you block out your days for a week, cut and place the colored stickies on the calendar to block as much time as you need for that heading each day.

Then, as you change the plan throughout the week, play the time-blocking game. Anytime you change your plan, make it a deliberate choice. If on Tuesday you decide to attend meetings all morning even though you had scheduled time to review the financials and write the quarterly report during that time, pull off the green "planning work" sticky note and replace it with a blue "meetings" sticky note. Now you have a green "planning work" sticky note in your hand that is the size of three hours. Where are you going to put it? Will you stay late, replacing the purple "family time"? Will you come in on Saturday, replacing the orange "exercise time"? Will you put off "responding to e-mails and calls" this afternoon and move that yellow sticky note to tomorrow morning and come in early? Every time you change your plan, you have to acknowledge that you now owe yourself that many hours for that heading, and you have to find a place for it or make a choice not to do the tasks on the list for that block of time.

When people fail to make conscious choices, they simply replace their planned work with unplanned demands and drop the planned work altogether. The sticky note exercise forces you to realize that anytime you choose not to do something, you have to find another time to do it. This process helps you maintain balance because you don't lose sight of what has to be done. It requires that you recognize you have only so much time and must say no to projects that don't support your plan.

Forcing yourself to make conscious choices is vital to organizing. At different points in life, you will make different choices. But if you avoid choices, they'll be made for you by default.

Even with a plan, there will still be things you don't get done. But you will be choosing what to do and what not to do instead of frantically trying to do everything and failing. Knowing what you are not going to do gives you further choices. Now you can discuss with your team how to approach those things. Will you decide to give up those projects? Hire additional staff? Delegate to others within or outside the department? Extend the deadline? Or adjust your priorities and do these projects instead of the ones you had initially decided to pursue?

Plan what you want to have happen at work and at home. *Purge* everything that doesn't relate to your plan. *Sort* your activities, as mundane as they may be. And then *place* them on your calendar so that you have scheduled time for each type of activity on a regular basis. Finally, *use* your system, making choices and adjusting your schedule as needed.

Project Planning

Any large project needs a deadline, whether internal or external. Without a deadline, it is hard to plan time to work on the project. That's why all those projects you're going to work on "when you have time" never get done. "When you have time" is like "later." It is a euphemism for "I'm not going to do that." If you're going to do it, identify or create the deadline, write it on the calendar, and then work backward from it.

Break the project down into smaller steps to make it more approachable and more manageable. Then identify how long each step will take and set minideadlines or milestones for each step. Put them on your calendar as well.

Finally, make appointments with yourself to accomplish each task. Write those appointments on the calendar, and respect them as you would respect an appointment with someone else.

Dealing with Interruptions

How do you take charge of your own calendar? During the course of the day, other people demand your attention. There are three ways to deal with interruptions: plan them into your day, plan them out of your day, or simply deal with them.

Plan them in. Plan into your day any interruptions you can anticipate. This allows you to deflect them when they occur inconveniently, rescheduling them for a more fitting time. Repetition of a similar type of request, complaint, or problem from family members, customers, or colleagues requires that you create a system to handle it. For example, schedule staff meetings frequently enough that basic issues can be handled in that forum. Employees will learn to count on that opportunity for communication and can then be discouraged from interrupting you.

Laura is the information technology officer of a large company. She has a broad range of planning and management functions but is also the company expert for computer problems. Every time somebody's computer has a problem, the person pops into her office, desperate for her help. Laura found she was falling far behind in all her other work. To be attentive to others' needs and still carve out time for her own work, she first posted a "Frequently Asked Questions" document on the company's server addressing the most common problems. Then she developed a form for people to fill out and e-mail to her when they were unable to resolve a problem independently. She reviews submissions five times a day and triages them, dealing immediately with urgent problems and scheduling the others for "fix it time," which she has planned into each afternoon. No employee has to go more than two hours without a response or more than twenty-four hours without direct support, but Laura is now able to plan hourlong blocks of time for her own work each morning. She reports, "I find I'm better able to solve people's problems when they have filled out the form because they are more thorough and rational than when they used to fly into my office in a frenzy." Laura has also found that people are more likely to solve their own problems.

Plan them out. Interruptions to plan out of your day are things that really shouldn't have happened in the first place. If poor planning or disorganization cause an interruption in your day, take the time to solve the problem so that it doesn't happen repeatedly. For example, put your keys in the same place every day so that you don't waste time looking for them. Establish clear standard work procedures so that employees can function without constant direction from you. Use your safe homes and time system consistently so that you don't lose notes or have to sift through piles to find what you need.

Karen has worked for the television studio for longer than anyone else. When she started, a number of other staff people routinely lost or misplaced critical pieces of equipment and inventory that Karen and the other producers needed. Over time, Karen collected and stockpiled her own inventory of necessary items. Because she couldn't trust other people to put things where they belonged, she acquired equipment of her own and kept it in her office.

Of course, everyone knew she had it, so when people couldn't find what they needed, they came to Karen. "Can I borrow the such-and-such?" Karen became the office inventory clerk. As the studio grew and Karen accepted a promotion, she continued to be the source for producers' equipment, as well as extra paper and pens, last year's phone book, and every other obscure item. When her office grew too crowded to work in, Karen began doing her work in the studio's lunchroom. And then she called me.

We identified the problem and purged from her office all the items she didn't use there. Next, we created a true inventory closet and inventory system to improve access to the equipment for everyone—with accountability for each individual. Now all employees can find what they need, staff members know who has what and for how long, and Karen can actually work in her office.

Don't fall into the trap of being the source because the workplace doesn't have appropriate systems. Create or improve the necessary systems to eliminate future interruptions.

Deal with them. If you choose to act on an interruption, give it your complete attention. First, look at your watch and decide how long you can allow for it. Put away what you're working on so that your space is open. Give the interruption your complete attention for the time you have allotted. If the issue is not resolved when the time is up, either summarize and refer it to another person or time or determine how much additional time is needed and check your calendar to confirm that you have that time to commit right now.

This response reminds the interrupter that he or she has interrupted you but also sends the signal that the person has your full attention for a period of time. It also allows both of you to be mindful of time so that you don't feel you've lost control of the day. You're making a choice to change your plan, not being dragged off course. By making active choices all along, deciding which problem will supersede the other agenda items you had for the day, you'll end the day still feeling productive and in control even if you changed your plan.

Getting Back to Work

Once the interrupter leaves, you face the most difficult aspect of the interruption: How do you get back on track with your day? Having your gears properly aligned will help. Following any interruption, reorient yourself with your lists and calendar to ensure that any activity that got displaced by the interruption is rescheduled for the future. By keeping track of what you have to do and consciously scheduling it, you'll be able to stay on track with your plan for the day and for your life.

Now, if you were gentle with yourself and didn't give yourself too much to do in any given day to begin with, you'll be able to find time in the near future for all the activities you just displaced. Recognize that every choice you make affects the projects you complete. Be aware of the choices you make, and use your lists and calendar to keep track of the actions you want to pursue.

Even if you work alone in an isolated setting and never answer the phone, you will probably have interruptions. In fact, people often create interruptions. So if it weren't for your coworker or clients or salespeople interrupting you, it would probably be the dog or the neighbor or the refrigerator causing a distraction. While it is important to allow time in your schedule to stretch, socialize, snack, and be human, try to avoid interrupting yourself with nonproductive worrying, frequent checking of e-mail or voice mail, and unfocused scrambling from one project to the next. Use your lists and calendar to plan each day, and use each part of the plan as a steppingstone to move you through your day.

Know what you can and can't control. Then take responsibility for your choices and let go of the rest. For example, you can control when you respond to phone calls. Choosing when you return calls places you in control because you can have the information in front of you and be ready to devote attention to it. However, you can't control an emergency—you simply have to respond. Yet even in that situation, consciously say to yourself, "I choose to respond to this. It will take about *x* hours," and then glance at your calendar and lists to see what that does to your day. Because your tasks are clearly outlined, you can redesign your day easily and still feel in control, even if your priorities have changed.

Overcoming Procrastination

Procrastination is avoiding doing something you don't want to do. If you know you're procrastinating, the problem is already half solved. Next, determine what you are avoiding and try to figure out why you are avoiding it. If you don't want to do it, maybe you shouldn't. Remember, simply choosing not to do something is one of the best ways to get it off your list.

Looking forward can help you overcome procrastination. Remind yourself of the outcome you're trying to achieve, and then act rather than react. Ask yourself what you have to do to take the next step with the project: Get help? Call someone? Write something? What do you have to do to jump-start the process? Look at each project as a series of smaller steps, and remember to take just one step at a time. Focus on getting it done rather than getting it perfect.

Remind yourself that you're moving toward a desired outcome, and state that *plan* out loud to help yourself see the end goal. *Purge* items on your "To Do" list that don't support your plan. *Sort* tasks based on activity to give you perspective and make it easier to put each task on your calendar. *Place* the activities on your calendar in blocks of time, and then keep these appointments with yourself. Say no to requests from others for the time you have blocked for yourself and your own projects. Finally, *use* the system, recognizing that you can't do everything and certainly not everything all at once. Reward yourself for projects you have completed.

By all means, let go of the guilt. Choose either to do the task or not. If you choose to do it, make an appointment with yourself. Put it on your calendar and get it done. If you choose not to do it, cross it off your list. Whether or not you choose to tackle the project, respect your decision and don't waste energy with further procrastination, with feeling guilty, or with second-guessing.

Multitasking

Modern computers can run several programs at once without sacrificing efficiency. The same cannot be said for humans. If you try to do more than one thing at a time, all the projects will suffer.

Teach yourself to focus on one project at a time. To do this, the following tasks are crucial:

- Create lists so that you can feel in control of all the tasks you face.

- Block time on your calendar for all the tasks and projects you need to pursue.

- Learn to deal with interruptions and procrastination.

- Don't interrupt yourself! Identify the task at hand. Then set parameters: "I will work on this until 11:00" or "I'll work on this until I have a rough draft finished." Then stay put and finish.

Realize, however, that even the most focused person needs to take breaks. Allow yourself to be human. It's better to respect your body's needs than to allow yourself to be distracted because you're longing to stretch your legs or get something to drink. After a short break, you can settle down again and focus on one project at a time.

8

Organizing Other People

One of the most common questions about organizing is, "What about my husband (wife, children, coworkers)?" People seem to feel that it is not enough simply to organize themselves; they want to organize other people too. They expect that as a professional organizer, I will agree.

I don't. You cannot organize someone else. And you shouldn't. Even as a professional organizer, I don't organize other people—I help people learn to organize themselves. Remember the definition of organizing presented in Chapter 1? Because organizing is personal, each person must define it for himself or herself; it is not one person's place to judge another as organized or not. Because organizing is a process, each person works at it daily at his or her own pace. And because organizing is the means to an end, each person decides for himself or herself whether more organization is needed to reach his or her goals.

You don't live in a vacuum, however. So to the extent that you share space or information and files, it is fair to have common ground rules. First, remember that organizing is not about appearances but about results. Everyone who uses the space (or information) should agree on the desired outcome. Everybody who shares the space—the family in the family room or the employees in the office space—and everybody who shares the information—the central filing banks—has to agree on the plan. What are you trying to accomplish? Focus on what you as a group or as members of the group have to do with the space or information. Everybody should be part of the plan.

Then, one person can be responsible for designing the system to keep space open and the stuff (or information) in safe homes. It is usually easier to have one person or a small team in charge of the *purge, sort,* and *place* steps based on the group's plan. After the person or team has finished setting up the system, everyone comes together again to see how the system works and agrees on any changes. Then everyone is responsible for using the system, whether it be for keeping track of client documents, reports, toys, or cooking utensils.

Remember that the purpose of organizing is to accomplish certain objectives. Appearances are not as important as function. Are you all getting done what you want to get done? If so, try not to judge what it looks like. If you want your home or office to be beautiful, organize first and then decorate around the system. Don't try to decorate first and then organize yourself into the picture. After you organize, you can accessorize or buy furniture or containers that reflect your style.

Finally, *use* the system yourself to model the behavior you want your coworkers (spouse, kids, others) to follow. Listen to their comments and concerns, and change the system as necessary when the needs of the group change. With a little patience, people with very different styles can function effectively with a well-designed system.

9
Backsliding

If, after you've established a system and used it for some time, you find piles starting to accumulate, don't be alarmed. Nearly everyone experiences some amount of backsliding from time to time. Backsliding—reverting to less organized habits, habits that jam the gears—is natural. It doesn't mean you have failed; it simply means you need to find out what caused the backsliding so you can correct it.

Backsliding usually occurs for one of six reasons:

1. The system is incomplete.
2. You have ignored the need for daily maintenance.
3. Events or activities have caused a temporary setback.
4. You are attempting to do too much.

5. The system is overly complicated.

6. You are experiencing a fundamental life change that is causing your goals to shift.

Backsliding often results when you go only part of the way toward setting up a new system, so beware of abandoning the process. This can happen easily; often the initial task takes several sessions to complete. Although it is important not to try to establish order all in one day, it is equally important to continue the effort once you start. Put appointments with yourself on the calendar at regular intervals to maintain the momentum once you have started. Organize all the spaces in your life, one by one. Create safe homes for all your stuff, and create links to your time system for what you have to do. Don't give up partway through the effort.

Backsliding is also common when the system is too complicated. If you find yourself avoiding putting stuff away or spending long periods of time planning and replanning your activities for the day, you may have created systems that are too complicated. Remember that organizing should be as simple as possible. Don't undermine yourself by making it harder than it has to be.

Sometimes you'll simply let systems slide because you are temporarily busier than usual. A vacation, holiday, or seasonal business rush can disrupt the normal patterns of your work or personal life, causing a temporary pileup. In this case, it is easy to solve the problem by scheduling just a little extra organizing time into the next day or two to catch up. This is the most common form of backsliding and the least worrisome. Organizing isn't about being perfect, so don't hold yourself to impossible standards. Go with the flow as long as you schedule time to catch up before the next rush begins.

On the other hand, when you assess the problem, you may discover that it is not the result of a temporary event but rather that you have ignored the need for daily maintenance. Remember that organizing is an ongoing process and that the last step to establishing any system is to *use* it. The solution, again, is scheduling. Write organizing time into each day, increasing the amount of time daily until you are able to maintain your space, stuff, and time effectively.

Suzanne runs a busy mail order business from her home office. The business is growing at breakneck speed. Though she has hired office help, there are many tasks that only she can do and numerous systems still evolving and changing that require her attention. She found it difficult to maintain organization on her own. To ensure that she made time to organize, she scheduled appointments with me for a set day each month. "I know at least once a month I'll have help and support to get the business back on track."

If you routinely feel your that days are too short to accomplish your goals or maintain your systems, either you have set too many goals or your systems are too complicated. Simplify and purge. Start by reapplying the Five Steps to Organizing Anything to your time gear, looking closely for actions to say no to. Then assess your stuff with a more ruthless eye—get rid of anything you don't truly use or love. Next, evaluate your space to be sure you have arranged it to help you work effectively.

Backsliding that results from a major life change is the easiest to identify because you start with the sentence "I used to be organized but then . . . ." Any significant transition—marriage, divorce, the birth of a child, the departure of a grown child, the death of loved one, a promotion or loss of your job—can permanently alter the way your gears intersect. When you can put your finger on a specific event during or after which the system broke down, you need to give yourself time to adjust your systems to connect with your current life. Set aside the time to reorganize space, stuff, and time whenever you experience a major life change.

Finally, be patient with yourself. All new skills take time to build. Use your systems, change them as necessary, and practice: organize every day, and every day will be organized.

10

You Can Do It!

When my oldest son was 3 years old, he got a tricycle and spent the entire summer trying to learn to ride it, without much success. He'd get so caught up watching the little pedals go around and around that he would veer off the sidewalk, down the little grassy knoll, and into the ditch every time. It was all I could do not to run after him yelling, "Look up, honey, look up." But I knew that with time and practice, he'd learn to look forward, balance, and build momentum to get where he wanted to go. Riding a tricycle is a skill that comes easily to some and harder to others, but anyone can learn.

Organizing is no different. All you need to do is learn the skills and then practice. With time (don't give up) and with practice (don't give up), you will begin to develop habits and systems that suit your work patterns and lifestyle. You've already taken the first step by buying this book. Congratulations! You're on your way.

Appendix
A

What to Save and How Long to Save It

This list provides you with general guidelines about what records a household typically needs to retain. Consult your accountant or attorney to confirm whether these guidelines are appropriate for you.

Financial Records

- ✓ Tax returns and supporting documentation—7 years
- ✓ Credit card receipts—discard after receiving monthly statement

- ✓ Credit card statements—1 year
- ✓ Check registers and canceled checks—1 year
- ✓ Deposit slips and ATM receipts—discard after receiving monthly bank statement
- ✓ Bank statements—1 year
- ✓ Investment statements—keep end-of-year summaries 7 years after close of account; discard monthly or quarterly statements when you receive end-of-year summary
- ✓ Investment purchase or sale confirmations and purchase records—7 years after sale of security
- ✓ Stock and bond certificates—keep in safe-deposit box as long as you own the security (see Appendix B)

Medical Records

If you itemized health expenses as a deduction on your taxes, keep records of insurance payments and direct medical expenses with tax records for 7 years; otherwise, discard after 1 year.

✓ Insurance policies—keep only most recent update of current policies

✓ Immunization records, operations, doctor, lab, and hospital reports—keep permanently

Household and Personal Documents

✓ All records pertaining to property (title, deeds, local tax payments, appraisals and assessments, mortgages, relevant correspondence) and receipts for major improvements—5 years after sale of property

✓ Inventories of furniture, jewelry, silver, furs, and collections of value—keep as long as you own the items; store inventory list in safe-deposit box with description, photo, and appraisal (see Appendix B)

✓ Utility bills—discard after 1 year (unless they are pertinent to a tax deduction, in which case you should keep with tax records for 7 years)

✓ Wills—update every few years; keep original in safe-deposit box, copy with attorney, copy at home

✓ Probate records (letters of appointment, inventory, decrees, wills)—3 years after closing estate; administrative expenses and final accounting—7 years after closing estate

Appendix
B
Your Safe-Deposit Box

Anything too valuable to be accidentally misplaced or destroyed by theft, fire, or natural disaster should be kept in a safe-deposit box at a bank. You may want to keep copies of all the items listed below at home in your files, but the originals belong in the safe-deposit box at the bank:

- ✓ Certificates of birth, death, marriage, and divorce
- ✓ Passports
- ✓ Stock certificates, bonds, and certificates of deposit. (The rental fee on your box is tax-deductible if it is used to store income-producing property such as bonds or stock certificates)

✓ Titles to property (including vehicles) and real estate

✓ Military discharge papers

✓ Mortgage papers

✓ Trust documents

✓ Pension plan

✓ Legal documents

The originals of the following items should be with your lawyer or executor, with copies in the safe-deposit box and at home. Do not store the originals in the safe-deposit box because the bank is likely to seal it upon your death.

✓ Copy of your will (with a note specifying the location of the original, usually with your lawyer)

✓ Copy of your letter of last instructions to your executor including the exact location of important documents, names and addresses of personal and legal advisers, and other relevant information

✓ Copy of a financial master list detailing all financial account numbers and contact names

Make a list describing all items in your safe-deposit box, and keep it in your file cabinet at home. Note that most safe-deposit boxes are not insured. If you store items of exceptional value, you may want to add a rider to your homeowner's or renter's policy providing the coverage you need.

Appendix

C

Organizers to the Rescue

If you find it hard to start getting organized, consider contacting a professional organizer. Professional organizers provide information, products, and assistance to help you organize to meet your needs. A professional organizer will guide, encourage, and educate you about basic principles of organizing by offering support, focus, and direction. The National Association of Professional Organizers (NAPO) offers organizers opportunities to sharpen their skills through ongoing education and professional development and has a code of ethics by which members are expected to abide. A professional organizer who is a NAPO member has made a commitment to his or her business and thus to you, the client.

You can find an organizer near you through NAPO's online referral system at http://action.napo.net/napo/referral. You can also contact NAPO in writing or by phone at:

National Association of Professional Organizers
35 Technology Parkway South, Suite 150
Norcross, GA 30092
Referral line: (770) 325-3440

With nearly two thousand organizers nationally, it is likely you will find one in your area.

Good luck and happy organizing!

Index

of e-mail, 61

of incoming materials, 46

of reading materials, 50

refusal

of incoming materials, 45 46

of reading materials, 50

renting vs. buying, 67

resource files, 75–76

retention, 40, 76–77, 116–122

RRRID list principles (e-mail management), 59–64

RRRIPP strategy, 44

for cluttered spaces, 18 19

for incoming materials, 44–47

for reading materials, 49–55

ruthlessness vs. recklessness, 37–38

safe-deposit boxes, 120–122

safe homes, 10, 70

scheduling time

for incoming materials, 47

for reading materials, 51

sequencing, 29

simple systems, 19–20

skim and pitch technique, 51

sorting

of activities on lists, 96

from lists, 92

of lists, 92

methods of, 25–26

space as organizing element, 8

space gear, 64–65

space maps, 69

sticky note exercise, 94–96

storage

maximization of, 67

offsite rental of, 67

stuff, 8, 66

surfaces, 64–65

tax deductions, 36, 43

tax records, 77, 117, 118, 120

time allocation, 85

time as organizing element, 8

time blocking, 94

time management, 84, 85

About the Author

After years of creating order out of chaos at the request of friends and family, Porter Knight founded *Organized by Knight* in 1996.

As a professional organizer, she has taught hundreds of clients to dig out from under piles and create systems to improve the flow of ideas, paper and the "stuff" we all accumulate in our lives. Porter is also a dynamic keynote speaker and seminar leader, providing organizing insights to audiences of all types and sizes.

Porter writes a monthly organizing column, airs a weekly radio show "Organizing On the Air," and has been featured in many publications and cable television channels. A graduate of Middlebury College (Middlebury, Vermont), she lives in Vermont with her husband and their two sons.

For other publications from

Visit our website at

www.discoverwriting.com